# Real C

# Oil Results

## Quick Start Guide to Losing Weight and Improving your Health the Natural Way

Donatella Giordano

NaturalWay
Publishing

Atlanta, Georgia USA

ISBN 978-1-491284-10-0

9 781491 284100 >

Copyright © 2012 Donatella Giordano

# Readers' Reviews

*"I never knew that eating fat could help me lose weight! And all the other benefits of this oil just blow my mind. I stumbled on a goldmine!"*

### ★★★★☆ Roger P. Hamilton – Salt Lake City

*"I can already feel a difference in my energy levels. Even my husband has commented on it! Thanks for writing such a complete and in-depth guide."*

### ★★★★★ Sandy Pickstone - Ontario

*"Coconut oil has now become a staple in our house and the children love it. I've lost some stubborn weight which didn't want to budge, by eating an oil! Who would have imagined?"*

### ★★★★★ Sarah Smith - Portland

Exclusive Bonus Download: Coconut Oil - The Healthy Fat

Coconut oil the complete natural health guide!

Find out the health benefits of coconut oil today!

Find out how coconut oil can, cure common illnesses saving you hundreds in doctors' fees, help you lose weight without losing the great taste of your favorite foods and much, much more!

Coconut oil has long been held in high repute by natural health specialists and doctors from a massively diverse range of countries. Western medicine has been slow to catch on to the health benefits of coconut oil but cutting edge research is finally catching up to what eastern doctors have known for centuries; COCONUT OIL IS GOOD FOR YOU!

Whilst many claims are made about the benefits of coconut oil in your diet and as a topical skin treatment finding good information on the wide range of benefits coconut oil can have for you can be incredibly time consuming and tricky.

**Download this guide and start improving your health NOW**

*Thank you for downloading my book. Please REVIEW this book on Amazon. I need your feedback to make the next version better. Thank you so much!*

## Books by Maggie Fitzgerald

Coconut Flour! 47+ Irresistible Recipes for Baking with Coconut Flour

Almond Flour! Gluten Free & Paleo Diet Cookbook

The Gluten Free Diet Quick Start Guide

Simple Gluten Free & Paleo Bread

Real Coconut Oil Results

www.amazon.com/author/donatellagiordano

# A Few Words From the Author

A lot of people think that coconut oil is not one of the best options available when it comes to cooking but they are wrong. I've written this book not only to prove that but also to help others discover the secrets of this special ingredient.

Going on a diet, most of the times, is not easy; going on a diet that actually works is even harder. I'm sure that you know a lot of people who went through heartache and pain to lose weight but didn't quite make it. Why did that happen? Probably because they followed the wrong diet, or perhaps because they were not determined enough to do it. A coconut oil based diet can help you lose weight without asking too much of you. All you have to do is follow the instructions.

In the pages of my book you'll find all you need to know about coconut oil and the ways it can help improve your physique, simple everyday exercises that will lead to a firmer body, tips and advice on food supplements and many more. So if you want to lose those extra pounds, improve your stamina and even your mood, you should read this book.

# TABLE OF CONTENTS

Disclaimer

While all attempts have been made to provide effective, verifiable information in this Book, neither the Author nor Publisher assumes any responsibility for errors, inaccuracies, or omissions. Any slights of people or organizations are unintentional.

This Book is not a source of medical information, and it should not be regarded as such. This publication is designed to provide accurate and authoritative information in regard to the subject matter covered. It is sold with the understanding that the publisher is not engaged in rendering a medical service. As with any medical advice, the reader is strongly encouraged to seek professional medical advice before taking action.

# Introduction

I've written a few health-related books before, and they've been focused on particular issues. I decided to try to do something different with this one, and focus on a specific food instead—and once I decided to do this, the choice of which food to write about was obvious. Coconut oil has become an absolute staple at my house, and I don't plan on ever going back to using any other kind of oil. But let me take a step back for a second.

When I sit down to write a book, I think about a certain need— what do people need to know about? What's been in the health news lately? What don't people understand? What do people have questions about? Recently, I've been getting quite a few questions about my decision to add coconut oil to my diet. People are concerned about the high amounts of saturated fat, and the links between saturated fat and heart disease—but what they don't know is that the picture is much more complicated than the food industry would have them think. There are a lot of misconceptions in the public opinion about coconut oil, and it's time that these misconceptions get cleared up. For this reason, I'm writing this guide to using coconut oil for weight loss. Of course, it has many more benefits than just helping you lose weight, but we'll get to that.

Throughout the course of this book, you'll learn a lot about various topics related to weight loss. First, about coconut oil, then about fats, then about the fats in coconut oil specifically. You'll also learn about the basics of weight loss and the ingredients that go into a successful weight loss plan. You'll learn how coconut oil and other coconut products fit into a successful plan, and why they're so much better than the other options out there. You'll learn how to do a successful detoxification cleanse of your body and start the diet plan. And finally, you'll see a number of recipes that will help you integrate this wonder food into your diet easily. Although you can use this guide as a sort of reference, and skip around to the parts that you want to read, I highly recommend that you read it in order, from front to back. Even if you think you know all that there is to know about weight loss, you're likely to learn at least a few things, and I think that really understanding the relationship between coconut oil, weight loss, and improved health is crucially important. Not only so that you understand why I recommend what I do, but also so that you can share this information with others. Coconut oil has gotten a bad rap, and it's time that someone stands up for it!

With that said, welcome to [title of book]. I hope that you enjoy it and find it useful, and I sincerely hope that it makes a difference in your weight loss efforts. We're all in it together!

Sincerely,

Donatella Giordano

# Allergy warning: contains coconut

Many people with allergies to tree nuts (like almonds, cashews, or walnuts) wonder if they can consume coconut-based products. This is a good question, but it doesn't have a simple answer. Coconuts are biologically similar to nuts, but they're not identical. Some people who are allergic to nuts are also allergic to coconuts, but others are not. If you have a nut allergy and you're interested in trying the coconut oil diet, discuss this first with your doctor or an allergy specialist so you can get tested before you start. Don't just start the diet and hope that your nut allergy doesn't also include coconuts.

# 1. Coconut oil: the basics

If you're like most people, you're going to start reading this book with a healthy dose of skepticism—*adding fat to my diet to lose weight? How is that possible?* And skepticism is good, because there are a lot of fad diets based on questionable science out there that start falling apart when you really question the reasons behind them. That's why I'm starting this book with a section about coconut oil and its benefits. Stay with me for a few sections, and you'll start to see why adding coconut oil to your diet is one of the best ways that you can add power to any weight-loss diet (you can even base an entire diet around it, like I've done in the last chapter of this book.)

Let's start with the basics. What, exactly, is coconut oil? Like it sounds, it's an oil that's extracted from coconuts—either the kernel or the meat. It's an unhydrogenated oil (if you're not sure what hydrogenation is, keep reading on), and it has a relatively low smoke point of 350 °F. When you first buy a jar of coconut oil, you may be surprised to find out that it has a very different texture than the one you're used to if you've been using vegetable or olive oils. Instead of being a liquid, it has a semi-solid texture, and often feels a bit grainy. But don't be put off by the slightly strange consistency—you can use it like any other oil. Its semi-solid state also makes it really great for using as a spread!

Coconut oil is produced in tropical areas; among the top producers of coconuts are countries like Brazil, India, Indonesia, and Sri Lanka. It's likely been consumed in these areas for thousands of years, both as a food staple and as a medicinal substance (which is why I always chuckle when people talk about coconut oil like it's a newly invented thing). Generally, coconut oil is used for the same kinds of things that other oils are, like cooking and baking, but you might be surprised to find out that there are actually quite a few other uses for coconut oil as well!

## 1.1 Know Your Fats

Before going into the details of the good things that coconut oil can do for your health, I should address a point that always, without fail, comes up in every discussion of coconut oil. Starting in the 70s and 80s, many people and groups started telling people to limit their consumption of coconut oil and other tropical oils due to their high saturated fat content. This led to what some people call the "tropical oil scare," which led to a significant drop in the use of these oils in the United States. People started using partially hydrogenated vegetable oils in place of tropical oils, and that continued until recently (you'll see why in a moment). Lest you fall prey to this scare, I'm going to get this question out of the way immediately. To really understand why the scare started and why coconut oil consumption should be *increased*, instead of decreased, you have to understand the difference between several different types of fats.

1. Saturated fats.

For several decades now, low-fat diets have been very popular, much to the detriment of the dieters who use them to try to lose weight in a healthy and permanent manner. These low-fat diets usually try to reduce all kinds of fat, but they especially focus on saturated fat, which is generally recognized as one of the types of fat that causes health problems. Saturated fat has been linked to atherosclerosis, heart disease, and other cardiovascular problems, and recent studies have uncovered possible links between saturated fat intake and increased risk of both cancer and bone problems. However, there's something very important to note here: there are *two* kinds of saturated fat. The first type, which most people are familiar with, comes from animal products, like meat and dairy. This is the saturated fat that's been used in most of these studies, and I won't disagree that this is a dangerous type of fat. Of course, if you consume it in reasonable amounts, you're almost certainly going to be just fine. But eating a lot of fatty meats and cheese could cause you some problems.

The second type of saturated fat is derived from plants, like the coconut. This type of saturated fat is chemically dissimilar to the fats that come from animal products. Yes, they're still saturated fats, but that doesn't mean that they have the same effects on the body. The reasoning behind this lies in the fatty acids that they're made of (fatty acids are the molecules that make up fats). Fats (triglycerides) are often classified based on how many carbon atoms they contain: short-chain triglycerides contain six or fewer carbon atoms, medium-chain triglycerides (MCTs) contain six to twelve carbon atoms, and long-chain triglycerides (LCTs) contain more than twelve. The primary fatty acid in coconut oil, lauric acid, is a medium-chain fatty acid, while the more common ones in the modern Western diet are long-chain ones—butter, for example, contains almost 90% long-chain triglycerides. These LCTs, because they are larger (even though this is on a tiny molecular scale), are more difficult for your body to break down, and often require pancreatic digestive enzymes and other substances produced in your digestive system, whereas MCTs are much easier to digest and don't require much, if any, help from organs outside of the stomach. This significantly reduces the amount of work that your body has to go through to get them into the blood stream where they're needed, meaning that they provide energy faster. LCTs, because they're more difficult to digest, are more likely to be stored as fat, and hang around in your body a lot longer.

After reading this, you may be wondering why, if they're so different, both of these fats are called "saturated." The reason lies in chemical naming nomenclature. I won't go into the details, but fats are "saturated" when there are a certain number of hydrogen atoms in the molecule that makes up the triglyceride. Because of this, both animal- and plant-derived fats can be classified as saturated, even though they're chemically different. If this confuses you, don't worry too much about it—it's not crucial to understanding that there's a difference between plant and animal fats. But if you're interested, you can find plenty of information about this online.

That's a lot of information to take in quickly, but it's good to know, because you're likely to have the experience, like so many others have, of someone saying "Coconut oil? You know that that's really high in fat, right? It causes heart disease!" By being able to explain the difference between MCTs and LCTs, you'll be better able make it clear to doubters that using coconut oil as a weight loss tool is not only healthy, but very effective.

2. Unsaturated fats.

This type of fat, in contrast, is generally considered to be much healthier. Unsaturated fats are also found in both animal and plant products, but you'll find more of them in oily fish, fruits and vegetables (especially fatty ones, like avocado), nuts, seeds, and other oils, including sunflower, canola, and olive oils. One of the fatty acids that make up some unsaturated fats is one that you may have heard of: omega-3. Omega-3s have gotten a lot of positive press in recent years due to their anti-inflammatory effect. I'll go into more detail about inflammation and why it's bad in the next section, but know that if you're trying to get more omega-3s into your diet, you're going to need to increase your intake of unsaturated fat (or take a supplement). Don't go overboard, though—even though they're generally associated with more positive things, like improving your blood cholesterol profile, having too many unsaturated fats is still bad for you. Even if you're having the right kind of fats, you can still have too many. Trying to keep your unsaturated-to-saturated ratio as high as possible is a good goal (using a food journal or a food-logging app like LoseIt! or MyFitnessPal is really good for getting information like this).

3. Trans-fats.

Unless you've been actively avoiding health news for the past decade or so, you've probably heard of trans-fats. Just to recap, though, here are the basics: trans-fats are unsaturated fats that are chemically different than other unsaturated fats. Something that many people don't realize is that these fats do occur in nature, but only in very small amounts. However, the food industry has been using man-made ones for a while, both as an alternative to tropical oils, and in other applications. Trans-fats are cheap, easy to work with, and are often used to alter the texture of other products (margarine, for example, uses trans-fats to help it stay solid at room temperature). To create trans-fats, companies add hydrogen to oils, which is why you've likely heard of "hydrogenated" or "partially hydrogenated" oils. If you see these words, you're definitely dealing with a trans-fat.

So what's so bad about trans-fats? If they're cheap, aren't saturated, and help keep food the right texture, what's the problem? The problem is that trans-fats are very strongly linked to a number of diseases, including coronary heart disease. Several studies have shown that trans-fat is the kind of fat that is most closely linked to heart disease, and that tens of thousands of deaths in the United States alone are attributable to trans-fat consumption *every year*. Trans-fats are taking a lot of the blame in the obesity epidemic, and might be linked to things like diabetes, liver dysfunction, and infertility. Obviously, this is not something you want to be putting into your body! Despite all the research showing that trans-fats are terrible things, they're still used quite a bit, and you'll find them in a lot of foods. If you only take away one thing from this book, it should be that trans-fats should avoided at all costs. The best thing you can do is to replace any oils that you currently have with extra virgin coconut oil, and you'll be sure that your oils are safe. You should still be checking the labels on the rest of your foods, though, as you might find them anywhere.

# 2. Benefits of coconut oil

As I mentioned above, the benefits of coconut oil are many; I'll be addressing the dietary ones here, and there are quite a few more that you'll find in the next section. Before I do that, though, I'll give a quick explanation of *why* coconut oil has these benefits. In an effort to keep this easy to understand, I'll be skipping over the hard science behind a lot of it, but if you do some research online, you should be able to find support for these claims without too much trouble.

In the last section, I discussed the difference between MCTs and LCTs. Recently, medical professionals have become more aware of the benefits of MCTs for the treatment of a huge number of diseases and conditions, including the following:

- Celiac disease
- Liver disease
- Gallbladder disease
- Digestion problems
- Cystic fibrosis
- Alzheimer's disease
- Seizures
- AIDS

Not only that, but MCTs are often used to help infants get the nutrition that they need when they're not feeding correctly, because they're such an efficient and healthy source of nourishment. MCTs do really great things for the body, and coconut oil is a fantastic source of these fats. Some people also recommend MCTs for the treatment of these issues:

- Athlete's foot
- Flu
- Hepatitis C
- Herpes
- Common cold
- Measles
- Streptococcus

There are very, very few problems that aren't likely to be at least indirectly helped by the addition of more MCTs into your diet. Of course, clinical evidence is equivocal, as it is in most cases, but scientists are continually researching and finding more evidence for the effectiveness of MCTs in treating various diseases. Either way, even the possibility of MCTs being able to treat this many conditions is something worth considering.

Second, it's important to understand the role that inflammation plays in the body. This is often one that's misunderstood, and I'd like to clear it up here. Inflammation is a good thing—*in the short term*. When your body is confronted with something that's not good for it, whether that's an injury, some sort of physical irritation, stress, or hard-to-process food, it releases inflammatory substances. When you have an acute injury, you'll see the signs of this inflammation right away—redness, swelling, and pain are generally the most indicative of an inflammatory response. This is the body protecting and healing itself, which is a good thing. However, when you're exposed to inflammation over a long period of time (chronic inflammation), there are some serious consequences. For example, when you're stressed out a lot, you can lose the ability to regulate cortisol, a hormone that controls the inflammatory process. And when you include too many inflammatory substances in your diet, your body's inflammatory actions get out of balance, sometimes with dire effects. Uncontrolled long-term inflammation has been linked to things like arthritis, asthma, diabetes, hay fever, heart disease, autoimmune disorders, cancer, and, importantly, obesity. Getting inflammation under control is one of the best things you can do for your health, and the cleanse that I recommend in chapter 6.1 is a great way to "reset" your body's inflammatory system. Including coconut oil in your diet, as well as taking an anti-inflammatory supplement, will also help.

Coconut oil also does a lot to get inflammation under control. It's not fully understood exactly how it does this, but it seems to help the body regulate the balance between inflammatory and anti-inflammatory substances. In addition to this balancing effect, coconut oil enhances the body's inflammatory response, meaning that when you actually *do* need the inflammatory substances in your body, they'll be more effective.

Two of the traditional indicators of heart health, blood pressure and cholesterol levels, are also improved by the addition of coconut oil to your diet. High blood pressure has long been known to be a risk factor for cardiovascular disease, and while the addition of coconut oil doesn't actively lower your blood pressure, it will likely replace other oils that are likely to *raise* your blood pressure. Hydrogenated oils have been linked to an increase in blood pressure, and you won't be using those anymore after you realize how great coconut oil is! The relationship between coconut oil and cholesterol is a complicated one, and there have been many studies both on the link between cholesterol and heart disease, and on the connection between coconut oil and cholesterol. However, a few things must be pointed out about some of the studies that have received publicity—first, not all of them used virgin coconut oil in their experiments. This is crucially important, because if they used a hydrogenated coconut oil, there's no doubt that it would raise cholesterol, and blood pressure, and have all kinds of negative effects. Second, some of the studies looked at total cholesterol levels, which can be misleading. There are two kinds of cholesterol: HDL, which is good, and LDL, which is bad. The HDL-to-LDL ratio is a very important level to monitor in the body, and if total cholesterol levels increase, that can actually be a *good* thing if it's the HDL that's going up. Studies have shown that coconut oil can increase HDL. So, while there's only marginal evidence that coconut oil is beneficial for blood pressure and cholesterol, there's no evidence that it has negative effects on either of these. And if you're replacing oils that will definitely have negative effects, you're making progress!

# 3. Uses of coconut oil

As I mentioned earlier, coconut oil is primarily used (at least in this diet) for cooking and baking. It can replace any oil that you're using for cooking at the moment, unless you're deep-frying--which you shouldn't be when you're on a diet. But in case you are, the low smoke point of coconut oil makes it a poor choice for deep-frying. Coconut oil does have some taste to it, so you may find that your favourite dishes have a bit of a new flavour, but it's something that you'll get used to. This can also encourage you to try new things, which is nice!

Cooking and baking aren't the only things that people use coconut oil for, however. One thing that many people find it useful for is as a replacement for their current lotion or skin moisturizer. Just rub a bit of it onto your face or any other area that need some moisturizing, and it'll be well-nourished and looking great in no time! You don't need to use very much. Also, you might note that it feels really greasy at first, but it will quickly absorb into your skin and start working its magic. If it feels grainy when you take it out of the jar, you can rub it in your palms for a moment to heat it up a bit and try to dissolve some of the grains before applying it. If you're looking for a cleanser, just combine coconut oil with your favourite exfoliant (like sugar), and you have an all-natural way to keep your skin clean and beautiful. I've also heard of using coconut oil as a replacement for shaving cream and as a makeup remover!

Like your skin, your hair can benefit from an occasional application of coconut oil as well. If you're looking to repair split ends, tame frizz, boost shine, or moisturize your scalp, just rub or brush some of the oil into your hair in the morning. I've also heard of creating a hair mask using coconut oil. Again, just use a little bit—it's easy to over-apply the oil, because a little bit can go a long way!

A few of the more unique uses that I've heard of for coconut oil include as a toothpaste when mixed with baking soda, and as an anti-aging cream when applied around the eyes. Katie, the woman behind the health blog Wellness Mama, even recommends using it as a diaper cream, a wound and sunburn salve, a treatment for lice, and a leather conditioner! (I highly recommend checking out her post "101 Uses for Coconut Oil"—it's fascinating.) Its versatility is a testament to how useful and beneficial it is. If it does good things for your skin, imagine how good it is for your overall health when you ingest it!

Before you go off and start using coconut oil for everything, I'd like to point out that not every coconut oil has the same benefits. Like most things, there are different grades of coconut oil, and it's important that you use the highest-quality product you can get. It's especially important that you use unrefined and unprocessed oil, as the additives, chemicals, and processes that food producers use to prepare this oil for the shelf significantly reduce its benefits and may make it more harmful. If you seek out virgin or extra virgin coconut oil, you'll be getting the most natural, raw product that you can get, and this is definitely what I recommend. Throughout the rest of the book, I'll be referring to coconut oil, but what I'm really talking about is virgin or extra virgin coconut oil.

# 4. Where to buy coconut oil

Now that you know all about coconut oil, you might be wondering where to find it. If you go to the corner grocery store, you might find that they have vegetable oil, and maybe some olive oil, and that's about it. To find coconut oil, it's possible that you'll have to look a little harder. One of the places that I go regularly for coconut oil, coconut milk, and coconut meat is an Asian grocery store. Coconuts are often used in Asian cuisines like Thai and Chinese, so if you live in an area large enough to have one of these grocery stores, you're in luck. If not, the next place I suggest looking is at mid-to-high-end grocery stores that tend to carry all-natural and organic foods. Places like Trader Joe's, Sprouts, and Whole Foods are good bets. Finally, if you can't find coconut oil anywhere else, you might check at a health foods store, like GNC or The Vitamin Shoppe (these might be somewhat more expensive than the previous stores). If all else fails, you can buy from an online retailer like Tropical Traditions or another similar website. And last time I checked, there's nothing you can't buy on Amazon. Keep in mind that if you're going to be paying for shipping, it might be worth buying in large quantities, either to store for later use or to split with friends or family.

# 5. Losing weight with coconut oil

*All of this is great,* you might be saying, *but how does it help me lose weight?* This is a guide about weight loss, after all, and I realize that the connections between the benefits I laid out in the previous section and losing weight might not be super clear. In this section, I'll first provide you with the basics of weight loss, and then go on to show you how coconut oil can help you meet your weight loss goals.

Before I go on, though, I just want to remind you exactly why losing weight is a good idea. I'm sure you already know most of these things, but keeping them in mind is great for staying motivated! And you might actually learn something here. So, first, of course, there's the aesthetic value of losing weight. Our culture places too high of an emphasis on being skinny, but being trim and healthy is very attractive. Now, I'm not trying to make any sweeping statements here, and I have to point out that being thin is *not* the only factor—or even the main factor—in attractiveness. But it's a very motivating thing for a lot of people, so it deserves mention.

Second, if you're currently over your ideal weight, you may find it difficult to do some things. Some people, for example, find it difficult to keep up with their kids after more than 10 or 15 minutes of running around in the park, and want to lose weight and improve their fitness at the same time. This is a great goal, and a lot of people have found that increased fitness is a great motivator, and that exercise is actually something that they enjoy a lot! You don't have to run a marathon or complete a triathlon to get more fit (though those are both great ways to do it), but just having a little bit more stamina is great when you're going on a long walk on an autumn day. That's a big reason why I try to stay in good shape.

Third, there are the health reasons. This is a really big deal, and contributes to a lot of people's weight loss motivations. Being overweight or obese is linked to a huge number of diseases and disorders, including cardiovascular issues like coronary heart disease, poor bone health, asthma, high blood pressure, cancer, back pain, ulcers, gallstones, and more. Sometimes it seems like there aren't any conditions that aren't in some way linked to obesity. Of course, the more overweight you are, the more at risk you are, so losing weight becomes even more important. Some of these diseases can be fatal, and many reduce your expected lifespan—and, of course, some are just plain unpleasant. So getting down to your ideal weight has the potential to significantly improve the quality (and the length) of your life.

Finally, there are healthcare costs. Healthcare has been in the news a lot lately, and most of it has to do with rising costs and insurance difficulties. I'm speaking from experience when I tell you that if you have any sort of health condition, it can be very difficult to get insurance, even if it's just a minor issue that's well-controlled. And once you do get insurance, you're likely to be paying a lot more for it. If you're on a group plan through your employer or your spouse's employer, you might be able to avoid these added costs, but with the economy as it is, it's hard to know how long these plans are going to last and what the options are going to be in the near future. Even if you're in pretty good health now and you have a good insurance plan, there's no guarantee that being overweight won't be costing you a significant amount of money in the coming years. And even if you're well-covered, you will be spending time in visits to the doctor, trips to the pharmacy, and potentially hospital time, all of which will take time away from the things that you need and want to do.

Of course, spending a long time in the hospital because of being overweight is pretty rare. The chances are, in fact, probably miniscule. But is it something you want to risk? Wouldn't you rather be happier, healthier, and at less risk? Then getting down to a healthy weight is the way to go. When you commit to losing weight, you should have a personal reason—something that really appeals to *you*—that keeps you going. If you don't have one yet, I encourage you to take a moment to think about it before going on.

## 5.1 Weight Loss Basics

Okay, do you have your weight-loss motivator in mind? Then you're ready for the basic principles of weight loss.

### 1. The calorie deficit.

If you know much about dieting, you know that the premise behind every diet is the calorie deficit—consuming fewer calories than you burn. If you consume *more* calories than you burn, you'll gain weight. If you consume less, you'll lose weight. There's no way around this. Diets work by decreasing the number of calories that you consume every day. Of course, diets propose to do this in different ways; some have you cut your calories significantly on certain days, others have you eat at certain times to optimize your metabolism, and others encourage you to eat certain foods that have weight loss benefits. Obviously, the problem with restricting your caloric intake is that you get hungry. And, if you're like me, you get really irritable when you're hungry all day. Not eating enough will also decrease your energy, making it difficult to make it through a normal day. Obviously, you need to balance these considerations against how much you restrict your calories. This is one of the most difficult parts of dieting, and not correctly balancing these two issues is behind almost every diet failure.

Of course, there's another side to the weight-loss equation—the calorie-burning side. To aid in establishing a calorie deficit, you can also increase the number of calories that you burn, usually through adding exercise. Exercise has all kinds of benefits in addition to helping you burn calories, including relieving stress, improving bone health, lowering blood pressure, and making you less likely to contract all sorts of diseases. But in the context of dieting, its big advantage is that it helps you burn more calories. However, with that increased calorie burning comes more hunger, which will make you want to eat more—your body needs to be fueled to exercise, after all. So, again, you're looking at creating a balance; this time, between increasing your calorie burning and increasing your calorie intake to cope with it. You can see why getting your diet and exercise exactly right is important.

## 2. Common issues.

These premises are pretty simple, but most popular diets tend to derail efforts at weight loss in a number of ways. First, many diets recommend that you cut out as much fat as possible from your diet. After reading about the benefits of the healthy saturated fats in coconut oil, I'm sure you can see why this is a bad idea. Not only that, but many so-called "diet" foods are high in unhealthy trans-fats and other chemical substances that can harm your body and make it harder to lose weight. As you'll see, we'll be cutting those foods out during the cleanse. Many diets also involve a restriction of calories that is so severe that the body actually goes into survival mode, which causes metabolism to *drop*, and storage of calories to *rise*, which is exactly the opposite of what you should be doing if you're trying to lose weight. So, between depriving yourself of essential nutrients and not consuming enough calories, you really throw your body out of whack—no wonder it's so hard to lose weight with these diets! And even if you do manage to lose weight with these plans, it's almost impossible to keep it off. These diets set you up for immediate success and long-term failure. They also often make you more vulnerable to chronic diseases.

The weight loss plan that I'll present in chapter 6.2 takes all of these factors into account and deals with them by recommending a balanced diet, a moderate calorie restriction, and healthy amounts of exercise. *These* are the basics of weight loss, not caffeine pills, magic water, eating only grapefruit, or fasting. It's all about balance.

## 3. What's my ideal weight?

This is a question that comes up a lot, especially when people start dieting. After all, when you start losing weight, you should have a goal to aim for (it's possible to go about it with the intention of just losing "some" weight, but this is really hard, and is tough to motivate yourself for). Unfortunately, it's not a very easy question to answer. There are a lot of formulas that you can use, and you can find them all online. One of the most standard ones is the body mass index (BMI), a number that was devised to estimate how close you are to your ideal weight. Here's the equation:

BMI = (weight (lbs.) / height (in.)2) x 703

You can also just use an online calculator. Anyway, a "normal" BMI is between 18.5 and 25, while overweight is 25–30, and obese is over 30. This is a good initial guide, but it's not always accurate. For example, there was a softball coach at my university who ran 6 miles just about every day and was a great weightlifter, but he was classified as overweight, because BMI doesn't take body composition into account. So BMI is a good place to start, but you may want to seek a more informed opinion once you get going. Where do you get an informed opinion on your ideal weight? A physician is a good person to ask, and a personal trainer could also probably give you a good answer.

### 4. How quickly should I lose weight?

Different people are able to lose weight at different rates, and this is actually affected quite a bit by the difference between your current weight and your goal weight. The further above your ideal weight you are, the more likely you'll be able to lose several pounds a week for the first few weeks. This is great, but I have bad news: it's not all going to come off that quickly. A lot of the weight that you lose in the first week or two of dieting is actually water weight, and can come back at any time. And due to hormonal cycles, life events, and other circumstances, you might find that your weight fluctuates as you go through your weight loss process. I know that when I'm trying to lose weight, I can go up and down as much as three or four pounds over the course of a couple days, but it takes longer than that to move solidly down the scale. What I'm trying to get at here is this: don't get discouraged! Losing weight is a process that can take a while, and requires discipline and commitment. Be patient, stick to your plan, and you'll get there. Don't be dismayed by setbacks—every dieter has them. Take them in stride, and move on.

That said, one pound per week is generally considered to be a safe and reasonable rate of weight loss. So if you're trying to lose ten pounds, you should be aiming to get to your goal weight in around two-and-a-half months. If you're trying to lose forty pounds, it will likely take you the better part of a year. And I know that this seems like a long time, but trying to go faster than this can cause problems, not only with your weight loss, but also with your health. If you speed through the first five or ten pounds and then discover that it's getting more difficult, you may find it hard to keep your motivation. So set a reasonable goal, take it slow, and you'll get there! Trust me. I hate it when people tell me this, but it's true: patience is a virtue.

## 5.2. The Role of Coconut

You may be wondering how coconut oil fits into this equation. Below, I've outlined the ways in which coconut oil, coconut milk, and coconut meat can all contribute to your weight loss plan.

### 1. Coconut oil.

One of the primary ways in which coconut oil can help you lose weight is by increasing satiety. Satiety is the feeling of "fullness" that you get after you eat. If you're satiated, you won't be hungry. Which foods contribute to satiety? Those with protein, fat, and complex carbohydrates, like those found in produce. The healthy saturated fats in coconut oil help you stay fuller longer, making you less likely to snack between meals. If you've ever been on a low-fat diet in the past, you've probably had the experience of serious sweet cravings between meals—this can often be the result of not having enough fat in your diet. By adding coconut oil to your diet, you'll help add staying power to your meals. You'll see that in the diet plan I present below, there's quite a bit of protein and complex carbohydrates as well. The MCTs in coconut oil are digested easily, which will also help you feel full without getting bloated, experiencing indigestion, or having any other of the very common problems in standard diets.

Another way in which coconut oil helps you lose weight is that it modulates the storage of fat in your body. First of all, it's more easily processed by the liver, so your body won't need to store it like it does with other kinds of oils. This is a huge benefit. Second, it helps keep your blood insulin levels in check, which is important because the amount of insulin in your blood has a direct impact on how much of your caloric intake is stored as fat. And by helping to keep it level, you'll avoid fat-storing spikes and drops. Finally, it helps reduce the amount of fat that's stored in and around your abdomen, which is not only unsightly, but also one of the most unhealthy areas to store fat (abdominal fat is strongly linked to heart disease).

In addition to helping your body store fat in the most efficient and healthy way possible, the MCTs in coconut oil have also been shown to increase your metabolism, which goes a long way toward establishing a calorie deficit, which, as I pointed out earlier, is the most crucial part of any diet. Your basal metabolic rate—the amount of calories your body burns at rest, just to keep itself going—is one of the main ways in which you burn calories throughout a day, and consuming coconut oil can help increase that rate, meaning you'll be burning more calories without doing more work! What more could you ask for?

Different experts and organizations give different recommended amounts of daily intake, but around four tablespoons seems to be good, so you should keep that as your goal. Four tablespoons is also a quarter-cup, so you can think about it that way if you prefer.

### 2. Coconut milk.

While coconut oil gets the most recognition, there are other ways to get the healthy substances that abound in coconuts. Coconut milk is one of my favorite ways to do this, as it's easily used as replacement for milk in many recipes, allowing you to both reduce unhealthy saturated fats and add a dose of healthy micronutrients and anti-oxidants to your diet. You can cook with it, bake with it, and even just drink it plain! Add it to your cereal or your tea instead of dairy milk, and you might find that you have absolutely no desire to go back. You can also make cream and whipping cream out of coconut milk, which increases its versatility.

Coconut milk is usually bought in cans, and you can buy either full-fat or light versions. I recommend going with the full-fat versions, even though they're higher in calories and saturated fat, because the saturated fats in coconut milk are the healthy kind, and they're behind many of the benefits of coconut products, especially for dieters. If you find that the full-fat version is a bit much for you, feel free to water it down. There are quite a few brands out there, but I recommend Thai Kitchen—you can get coconut milk from them in either regular or organic. While they're both good, I recommend the organic, as it's free from pesticides and other additives that can have adverse health effects.

### 3. Coconut meat.

Coconut meat, or coconut flesh, is the white part from the inside of the coconut (yes, I know it's weird to call it "meat" or "flesh," but that's just what it's called). Like the previously mentioned coconut products, this also contains the MCTs, micronutrients, and anti-oxidants that are so beneficial to your health. It also contains fiber that will help keep you full and clean out your digestive system. There are a lot of great uses for coconut meat, including using it in smoothies and shakes, baking it into pies, eating it raw, and adding it to parfaits. Of course, you can find hundreds of recipes that include coconut meat online, and I've included several at the end of this book that you can use as well. If you've never had raw, fresh coconut, though, I highly recommend trying it! Just scoop some out of the shell and eat it with a spoon.

Speaking of the shell, there are a few ways in which you can buy coconut meat, but the most common are canned or in a whole coconut. Canned meat is easy to deal with—just open up the can, drain it, and use it for whatever you'd like. Cracking open a raw coconut and extracting the meat is slightly more involved, and I won't get into it here. (There are plenty of videos online that'll show you how to open a coconut.) If you decide to use a whole coconut, you can also drain the water from the inside first and use that in your cooking as well! Of course, cracking open a coconut takes some force, so be careful if you take a shot at doing this. That said, it's really fun to open up a coconut! I think everyone should do it at least once.

# 6. The coconut oil weight loss plan

In this section, I'll detail my 21-day plan to lose weight with coconut oil. It starts with a 7-day cleansing period, during which you'll cut out a lot of harmful foods from your diet and help your body reset to its natural state. After that, you'll use the following 14 days to adjust to the diet itself. And after the initial 21 days, you'll be set to continue your weight loss until you reach your goal weight! Of course, there's a lot more to losing weight than just adding coconut oil to your diet, so I'll address the other things that you need, as well.

## 6.1. Coconut Oil Cleanse

The cleanse or "detox" phase is an important part of dieting, but it's one that's often neglected. What many people don't realize is that there are hormonal imbalances that are created by eating a normal Western diet, and that these imbalances can hinder your weight loss efforts. As long as you continue to eat those foods, your body will stay in a state of imbalance, which causes inflammation, one of the causes of unhealthy weight gain. So why not cut them out gradually, you might ask? Well, first, it's really hard to do that. We've become addicted to many of the substances that are found in pre-packaged, processed foods, and cutting them out over a period of time is hard. You'll deal with cravings, and backsliding, and difficulty when you cut out a second food, and so on. It's best to just get it all done at once. Second, even when you're in the primary phase of the diet, you'll still be consuming a few of the unhealthy fats and chemicals that you're trying to cut out. That's just how life goes. There are very few people who have the time, money, and energy to eat all organic food all the time. And so if you try to cut these foods out gradually, but you're still consuming others, it's only going to be mildly effective. Overall, it's just going to be better to do it all at once. When your body gets into detoxification mode, it starts flushing out toxins, and you want to do everything you can to help it.

And I want to be clear about this: there are definitely harmful substances in the foods you eat every day that you want your body to get rid of. Trans-fats, genetically modified substances, pesticides, antibiotics, hormones, preservatives . . . the human body was not meant to be consuming these things, and we still aren't totally clear on their effects (even if the food industry tells you they understand them). Many people think that the substances you'll be flushing out are to blame for many modern diseases, including hypertension (high blood pressure), coronary heart disease, type II diabetes, and cancer. Whether or not this is true, or can be proven, is tough to tell. But what *is* true is that cultures that don't consume these substances are generally a lot healthier, live longer lives, and don't suffer from these kinds of conditions. A lot of these cultures have also been using coconut oil for hundreds, if not thousands, of years, so . . . you can draw conclusions for yourself.

I'm going to be honest with you—going through a cleansing phase isn't easy at first. You'll definitely get used to it, and it will become a lot easier, but you may not enjoy it very much for the first few days, and maybe even the entire week. As your body is ridding itself of toxins and re-balancing its various systems, you might feel fatigued, get headaches, or have some trouble with digestion. All of these are normal, and should resolve pretty quickly. If you find that going through a cleanse is really hard on your system, you might consider extending it to two weeks and only cutting out half of the harmful foods during the first week, so your body gets a chance to acclimate itself to these changes. But don't take some discomfort as a sign that you shouldn't be cleansing—just know that your body has become accustomed to a lot of pretty awful substances over the years, and it's not going to be easy to get rid of them. But it'll get better, I promise.

Another thing that I like to recommend is to do repeated cleanses throughout the year. I usually do a one-week cleanse three or four times per year and one two-week cleanse each year. Some people do a lot more than this, but I think this is a pretty reasonable expectation. By cleansing your body on a regular basis, you'll help it stay healthy by not allowing toxins to build up. Even if you're very careful about your diet, it's likely that you'll be consuming at least a few harmful substances every once in a while, and this can add up over time; cleansing will keep it from getting to harmful levels. Of course, if you adopt a gluten-free, totally organic diet with no table sugar or processed food, you might not have to worry about cleansing often. But most people can't commit to a diet quite as stringent as that, so I recommend cleansing.

Below, I've enumerated the four most important steps you can take during a cleanse. There are as many cleanses as there are diet programs, so if this plan doesn't work for you, you can definitely find one that does. Also, I consider this to be a pretty moderate cleanse. If you feel like you want more cleansing power, you can cut more foods out of your diet; just don't cut too many, or you run the risk of not consuming enough calories, which will hamper your weight loss efforts.

**1. Adequately prepare for your cleanse.**

Because a cleanse is a week-long (or two-week-long) health commitment, it pays to be prepared. It's hard to just jump into a detoxification period without doing anything leading up to it. In the week or few days before your cleanse, I recommend making an effort to just "eat healthy" when you can. Don't make any specific goals, just skip dessert sometimes and choose a vegetarian dish over a meat-containing one a few times a week. Start cutting out caffeinated and sweetened drinks so you don't go through a withdrawal period when you start your cleanse (caffeine headaches are awful). It can be really helpful to try to put off grocery shopping until right before your cleanse week, so most of the disallowed foods will, for the most part, have been eaten and won't be tempting you (this is really easy to do if you have teenagers!). You can also be sure to stock up on the foods that you should be eating during the cleanse. Finally, invest in a nice water bottle that's visually appealing—you're going to have it with you constantly throughout the week, and likely longer than that, so buy something that's fun!

## 2. Eliminate harmful foods.

This is the most important part of the cleanse. Below is a list of foods that you should avoid during the entirety of the cleansing week—these are foods that have harmful substances (some natural, some man-made) that will keep you from effectively and permanently losing weight. If there's something that you absolutely can't live without, you can keep it in your diet, but I highly recommend restricting it as much as possible. I certainly understand that a cup of coffee can be a lifesaver when you're working on a deadline and your boss is breathing down your neck, and I occasionally indulge in one, but I'm careful not to make it a regular habit. Here are the foods, as well as some recommendations on what you can replace them with:

- Gluten-containing grains (wheat, rye, barley)—replace with non-gluten grains like chia and quinoa.*
- Red meat—replace with lean poultry or fish.
- Dairy—replace with hazelnut or almond milk, and use sheep or goat cheese if needed (keep to a minimum).
- Table sugar—you can probably live without this, but if you absolutely need something sweetened, you can use a tiny amount of honey or stevia.
- Very salty foods—use herbs instead of a huge amount of salt or spices in your cooking.
- Alcohol—you should just cut this out, but if you absolutely need something, stick with red wine.
- Caffeine—if you need an energy boost, try snacking on some vegetables with organic peanut butter.
- Artificial sweeteners—these are awful, and you should avoid them not just during the cleanse, but always.**
- Processed foods—replace with whole, fresh, unprocessed foods (by doing your own cooking and not using pre-

prepared or pre-packaged meals, you'll have taken care of this).

\* If you're asking why gluten is on this list, it's because the human body has not evolved to process it efficiently, and it may be linked to increasing inflammation.

\*\* Artificial sweeteners are found in sugar-free products like diet soda and sugar alternatives like NutraSweet, Equal, and Splenda. Some of the most common ones are aspartame, acesulfame potassium (also known as "acesulfame K"), and sucralose.

This is a relatively short list, but it contains a lot of the foods that are common in the American diet. Once you've gotten rid of gluten, excess sugar, and excess salt, you really don't have much left other than fresh produce and lean meats! That's the point of the cleanse— you're focusing on foods that your body is able to use efficiently and that haven't been saturated with toxic chemicals.

### 3. Replace all oils with coconut oil.

This isn't called the coconut oil diet for nothing! I've spent the first half of this book describing the benefits of coconut oil, so you should understand the reasoning behind this one really well by now. In cooking and baking, just replace any vegetable oil or other tropical oil with coconut oil. You can also use it to flavor foods or decaffeinated tea—some people even mix it into a glass of water to make sure they're getting a couple servings of it every day. No matter how you do it, make sure you're getting the beneficial medium-chain triglycerides from coconut oil, and get rid of any other oils you might be using.

### 4. Drink a lot of water.

I'm not going to tell you to drink eight 8-ounce glasses a day, or give you a formula that requires your age, weight, and astrological sign. Just make sure you're drinking a lot of water. And I mean *a lot*. You should be sipping on a glass or a bottle of water pretty much all day. This extra water intake will not only keep you hydrated, which is important for proper functioning, but it will also help your body flush out the toxins that it's become accustomed to over the past decades of unhealthy eating. This is of crucial importance—don't forget it!

If you follow these four guidelines, your body will be well on its way to detoxification in seven days. Of course, eating foods that have been exposed to pesticides, hormones, and preservatives for decades means you won't be able to completely clean out your body in a week. You can get a really good start, though, and by going through other cleanses throughout the year, you'll do yourself a big favour.

Finally, if you're looking for a more intense cleanse, you can also cut out things like starchy vegetables (potatoes, beans, corn), fruit juices, and soy products. Once these are out of your diet, you'll *really*only have the healthiest options left.

## 6.2. Coconut Oil Weight Loss Plan

Once you've completed the seven-day cleanse (congratulations!) you're ready to start the actual diet plan. Before I get into the specifics, however, I'd like to give you a note of caution about the week after the cleanse. After detoxifying your body, it's a good idea to not add all of those foods back into your diet at once. I know you're going to want to have a big cup of coffee and a burger to celebrate the successful cleanse, but it's best to just add one food back in at a time. This is a good way not only to make sure that your system is ready to go back into normal dieting mode, but also to find out if you have any food sensitivities that you weren't aware of. If you've added red meat and caffeine back in, but you start having some digestive trouble after adding dairy, you'll know that your body doesn't deal well with dairy products. A lot of people find out that they're slightly intolerant to something this way. Of course, I recommend that you keep all of those foods out of your diet all the time, but I know that isn't realistic for everyone. I give some recommendations below on the foods that I most strongly recommend keeping out of your diet.

I've split the diet plan into 7 different points to make it easier to read about. These are not presented in the order of importance, so don't think that the last few points aren't as important as the first ones. It's only presented in this way so it's easier to read.

## 1. Monitor your calorie balance.

As I mentioned before, the calorie equation is pretty simple: if you consume more than you burn, you'll gain weight. If you burn more than you consume, you'll lose weight. There's absolutely no getting around that. So it's a good idea to monitor your calorie intake. I know it sounds hard, and on some days it's not a lot of fun, but over time it gets easier, and it's really one of the best tools, if not *the* best tool, for losing weight. You can do this in a number of ways, but I recommend using the online food-journal service LoseIt!, which you can find at www.loseit.com (there's a paid option, but I've always used the free version). They offer a huge database full of foods that already have dietary information ready to go, and you can add any custom foods that you don't find there. You can also add commonly used recipes, which is a really handy feature, and LoseIt! helps you estimate the number of calories that you burn from exercise, giving you an accurate picture of your overall calorie balance. You can get LoseIt! for iOS and Android, so you can immediately enter foods on your phone.

Of course, you may prefer to just use an old-fashioned food journal—this is certainly the best choice for many people. If you're going to do this, you'll need to know how many calories you should eat each day. There are a lot of different equations out there, but one that's been around for a long time is this one, which provides two different formulas for men and women:

Women: BMR = 655 + (4.35 x weight (lbs.)) + (4.7 x height (in.)) - (4.7 x age (years))

Men: BMR = 66 + (6.23 x weight (lbs.)) + (12.7 x height (in.)) - (6.8 x age (years))

This approximates your basal metabolic rate (BMR), or the number of calories that your body burns at rest. You can then multiply this number by a factor depending on how active you are to get a total average calorie expenditure for a day:

- If you are sedentary (little or no exercise), use BMR x 1.2.
- If you are lightly active (light exercise or sports 1–3 days/week), use BMR x 1.375.
- If you are moderately active (moderate exercise or sports 3–5 days/week), use BMR x 1.55.
- If you are very active (hard exercise or sports 6–7 days a week), use BMR x 1.725.
- If you are extra active (very hard exercise or sports, a physically demanding job, or training 2x/day), use BMR x 1.9.

Once you've gotten your total for the day, all you have to do is consume fewer than that number and you'll start losing weight! A good goal is to establish a 500-calorie deficit each day of the week. This will lead to about a pound of weight loss each week, which is considered a safe amount to lose.

Of course, if you're one of those fantastically lucky people who don't need to count calories to lose weight, congratulations. We're all very jealous of you.

## 2. Exercise.

Obviously, restricting your calories only addresses one side of the calorie equation—the intake side. And while you *can* lose weight successfully by just restricting calorie intake, it's not easy. To most effectively lose weight and keep it off, you'll also have work on the other side by burning more calories. And while maximizing your calorie burning by adjusting how you eat will get you part of the way there, the best way to burn calories is most certainly exercise. Many people get nervous when they start thinking about exercise; they think that they're going to have to work super hard and be really uncomfortable and in pain for a long time without getting much out of it. However, I want to assure you that this is a misconception about exercise! Adding any form of exercise to your daily routine will help you burn calories; you don't have to become a fitness superstar.

For example, walking is actually one of the best forms of exercise for weight loss. Even if you don't feel like you're getting a great workout when you're out for a walk, you're actually improving your fitness just by doing it. An extended period of walking (like a 30-minute walk around the local park) increases your heart rate, even if you don't feel it, and helps get your calorie-burning system fired up. Walking uses the large muscles in your legs, as well as the stabilizing muscles in your abdomen, back, and hips, and helps strengthen all of those muscles, which is good for your posture and spinal health. And because you're standing and supporting your own weight, walking on a regular basis is good for your bone health (which is especially important for women who are near menopause, as they are at greater risk of osteoporosis). Didn't know that walking was so good for you, did you?

Of course, there are plenty of other exercise options if you don't like walking, or if you're looking for something slightly more intense. The important thing is that you're exercising in some way or another. The Centers for Disease Control and Prevention suggest at least 2 hours and 30 minutes of moderate-level aerobic activity every week (for their full recommendations, see Figure 1 below). What counts as moderate-level activity? The CDC recommends brisk walking, water aerobics, bike riding, playing doubles tennis, and pushing a lawn mower as activities that count for this level. How long you spend doing each activity at this level isn't as important as the overall weekly goal, as long as you're doing at least 10 minutes at a time. So if you go for a 10-minute walk three times a day, five days a week, you'll make it to the 2 hours and 30 minutes! The CDC's exercise guidelines also say that you can do 1 hour and 15 minutes of vigorous activity per week instead; these activities are things like running, biking fast or on hills, swimming laps, and playing basketball, singles tennis, or other sports. In addition to aerobic exercise, you should also be doing muscle-strengthening activities, like lifting weights, using resistance bands, body-weight exercises, or yoga, twice a week. If this all sounds like way more exercise than you're used to, don't worry—you don't have to go from no exercise to exercising every day.

## For Important Health Benefits

**Adults need at least:**

2 hours and 30 minutes (150 minutes) of moderate-intensity aerobic activity (i.e., brisk walking) every week **and**

muscle-strengthening activities on 2 or more days a week that work all major muscle groups (legs, hips, back, abdomen, chest, shoulders, and arms).

### OR

1 hour and 15 minutes (75 minutes) of vigorous-intensity aerobic activity (i.e., jogging or running) every week **and**

muscle-strengthening activities on 2 or more days a week that work all major muscle groups (legs, hips, back, abdomen, chest, shoulders, and arms).

### OR

An equivalent mix of moderate- and vigorous-intensity aerobic activity **and**

muscle-strengthening activities on 2 or more days a week that work all major muscle groups (legs, hips, back, abdomen, chest, shoulders, and arms).

## For Even *Greater* Health Benefits

**Adults should increase their activity to:**

5 hours (300 minutes) each week of moderate-intensity aerobic activity **and**

muscle-strengthening activities on 2 or more days a week that work all major muscle groups (legs, hips, back, abdomen, chest, shoulders, and arms).

———— *OR* ————

2 hours and 30 minutes (150 minutes) each week of vigorous-intensity aerobic activity **and**

muscle-strengthening activities on 2 or more days a week that work all major muscle groups (legs, hips, back, abdomen, chest, shoulders, and arms).

———— *OR* ————

An equivalent mix of moderate- and vigorous-intensity aerobic activity **and**

muscle-strengthening activities on 2 or more days a week that work all major muscle groups (legs, hips, back, abdomen, chest, shoulders, and arms).

Figure 1: The CDC's exercise recommendations.

(http://www.cdc.gov/physicalactivity/everyone/guidelines/adults.html)

No matter how you work exercise into your schedule, I strongly encourage you to find something that you enjoy doing. If you don't like going to the gym to get on the elliptical machine, go outside and take a walk or go for a bike ride. If exercise is a chore, you're much less likely to want to do it, and that can make the weight loss process a whole lot harder. I'm a firm believer in the idea that there's an exercise or a sport for everyone, and that finding it just takes some time. So get out there and start looking!

### 3. Adjust your eating to maximize calorie burning.

Your basal metabolic rate is one of the primary sources of calorie burning in your dieting process, so it's important to make sure you're getting every bit out of it that you can. Obviously, your body only needs so many calories, and you can't make it start using twice as many overnight. But there are a few strategies that will keep your body burning calories even when you're resting, and this can add up to a lot of calories over time!

First, make sure to eat breakfast. This is something that's neglected by a lot of dieters, much to their detriment. Having a healthy breakfast that contains both protein and fat helps get your metabolism up and running for the day, meaning that you'll be burning more calories all day. If you skip breakfast, you're also much more likely to overeat at lunch. And research has shown that eating breakfast makes it easier to stay focused and be productive in the morning, which is a great benefit that pays off even more if you're trying to get a workout in before work (or on a weekend morning before your family is up and about). Protein revs up your metabolism quite a bit, so having some with breakfast is a good idea—eggs or lean cuts of meat (I love turkey sausage with breakfast) are good, and are filling as well as metabolism-boosting, providing even further benefits. It can be harder to get breakfast protein if you're a vegetarian, but having a protein shake or making a smoothie and adding protein powder is definitely an option that you should consider.

Breakfast isn't the only time that it's important to have protein, though—whenever you have it during the day, it will serve to keep your metabolism going, so make sure that you're getting your protein intake throughout the day and not having it all at dinner. A couple slices of lean deli meat with cheese and fruit is a great afternoon snack, and will help fuel you to make it through the afternoon energy slump. Peanut butter is one of my favourite sources of protein, and it's also pretty filling, making it another good snack. Experiment with different sources of protein to see which you like best, and use them throughout the day to keep your metabolism revved up.

The last tip that I have to offer about upping your basal metabolism isn't actually a dietary tip, but is more related to the previous point on exercise. Muscle, when at rest, requires more calories than fat. Which means the more muscle you have, the more calories you're burning at rest. So get out there and build some muscle! Even light weight training can help increase your lean muscle mass. I know that a lot of women shy away from weight training because they don't want to "bulk up," but this is a bit of a myth. Women, because of several biological factors, are always going to be smaller than men, even if they lift a lot of weights. You can build a lot of muscle without looking bulky, and, as I mentioned earlier in the book, being trim and fit is quite flattering. If you've never done any weight training, I strongly encourage you to try it. You might like it a lot more than you expect!

### 4. Make coconut oil a mainstay of your diet.

It's likely that, if you've tried to lose weight in the past, you've already heard a lot of the suggestions that I've put forth in the previous sections. I hope it hasn't bored you, but in case you're one of those people who has heard it all before, here's something new: use more coconut oil! I won't go into all of the benefits here, because they've already been laid out in chapter 2. To make a long story short, I'll just present the highlights.

- The medium-chain triglycerides (MCTs) in coconut oil are easier for your body to digest and use, making it a very efficient fuel source—much more so than the long-chain triglycerides (LCTs) that are common in most of the other oils that you've been using in the past. This means they're less likely to cause any sort of indigestion or gastric distress, which can throw off the eating habits you're working so hard to maintain.

- Coconut oil can help you rebalance the anti-inflammatory and inflammatory substances in your body, which will help you use fat more efficiently. The right amount of cortisol, the hormone that's linked with a lot of inflammation, helps your body use its fuels well and keeps your from storing extra calories in the abdominal area.

- You'll be benefitting your overall health in several ways—for example, by reducing the risk of coronary heart disease, other cardiovascular issues, liver dysfunction, celiac disease, and possibly even more serious issues, like AIDS. When you're not combating these health problems, you're much more likely to be able to concentrate on and succeed at your weight loss.

And the list goes on--if you need to refresh your memory, see chapter 2.

To give you some ideas on how to get more coconut oil (and other coconut products) into your diet, I've included a number of recipes at the end of this book. Remember: aim to get around four tablespoons of coconut oil a day to enjoy the benefits. If all else fails, you can always stir a spoonful of it into your tea!

### 5. Add satiating foods to your diet.

If you're not familiar with the word "satiety," it's the feeling of fullness that you get when you eat—when you're satiated, your body is telling you to stop eating. Obviously, this is a very important signal that will keep you from overeating. However, there are many ways in which we sabotage this signal, causing us to keep eating after we've reached the point where our bodies don't require any more calories, which is what leads to weight gain. One of the ways in which you can take advantage of your body's satiety signalling system is to make sure that you're eating foods that aren't working against it.

One of the most important concepts in the discussion of satiety is the glycemic index (GI). This has been getting more attention in the dieting community lately, but a lot of people haven't realized that understanding it can be one of the key factors that helps you lose weight. When you consume food, it's converted into sugars that then enter your blood stream and are delivered to your muscles and organs; when your blood sugar levels are low, you get hungry. Once you've eaten, the levels rise, and your body stops sending you the "hungry" signal. When you have sugary foods, your blood sugar rises really quickly, and then drops again, causing a hormonal reaction that makes you hungry again. If you eat another sugary food, this cycle continues, causing you to consume way more calories than your body needs. And it's not just candy and soda that fall into the "sugary" category when it comes to the glycemic index. Things like white bread, some fruits, refined pasta, white rice, and dates are actually quite high on the glycemic index, meaning they cause a sharp rise in your blood sugar.

To avoid this cycle, you should try to replace foods that are high on the scale with foods that are low on it. If you look at foods that are low on the scale, you'll notice that they have some things in common: they're almost always either high in protein or high in fiber. These are the macronutrients that slow down nutrient absorption in your stomach, causing a more steady rise in your blood sugar. All of this may sound like complex biochemistry, but it actually makes a lot of sense. Think of the foods that keep you full for a long time when you eat them; they're the foods that you'll find are low on the list. Now you just have a better understanding of why that's the case.

| Food | Glycemic index |
|------|----------------|
| Instant rice | 87 |
| Brown rice | 55 |
| Spaghetti | 41 |
| Whole-wheat spaghetti | 37 |
| Baked potato | 85 |
| Sweet corn | 55 |
| Carrots | 49 |
| Bagel | 72 |
| Sourdough bread | 52 |
| Whole grain pumpernickel bread | 46 |
| Oatmeal | 61 |
| Potato chips | 54 |
| Rice cakes | 82 |
| Peanuts | 14 |

Figure 2: the glycemic index of some common foods

The scale above only includes 14 foods, but every food has a GI value. If you're not sure about the GI value of a particular food, you can look it up online, such as at glycemicindex.com.

### 6. Drink a lot of water.

I mentioned this in the previous section on cleansing, but I'll repeat it here because it's so important. In the context of weight loss, its most important function is probably to keep you full longer. By having a big glass of water before every meal and snack (and several other glasses throughout the day), you'll be filling up your stomach with a calorie-free liquid that's good for you in all kinds of ways. Definitely better than having a soda or a glass of juice!

### 7. Manage stress.

Most diets neglect to mention stress management as a weight loss technique, but I'm a strong proponent of including it in any dietary plan. Many people understand that stress changes their eating patterns—some people eat a lot when they're stressed, some people don't eat enough—but there's more to it than that. In addition to creating cravings for foods that usually aren't very good for you (when I'm really stressed, I go for macaroni and cheese!), stress has some physiological effects that you might not be aware of. For example, earlier in the book I mentioned cortisol, which, when it's present in large amounts, causes the storage of more body fat around the abdomen, which is unsightly and unhealthy. If you're stressed out a lot, your body loses control of its cortisol regulation systems, meaning that you'll have way too much of it moving around your bloodstream. So even if you're eating well, if you're highly stressed on a regular basis, you might still have problems getting rid of those last few pounds.

People have written entire books on stress management, so I can only give you the bare bones here. Everyone responds to stress-fighting tactics differently, and everyone has their preferred method of relaxation. But *you need to relax.* I can't stress how important relaxation is in stress management and weight loss. Only you know what you need to do to keep your stress at a manageable level, but I can offer a few suggestions. First, take some time for yourself and go somewhere. You can go on a weekend get-away with your friends, or spend a day hiking in the mountains, or even just take a few hours to go to your favourite coffee shop and read a book. Whatever you do, make sure it's something that you enjoy and that calms you. (Of course, just because something is calming doesn't mean it's mellow; many people are calmed by a good, hard run.) Second, make time to do this activity regularly. If you only take a day for yourself once a year, you're not going to make a dent in your stress levels. Once a week would be ideal. Twice a month is acceptable. But you should really be aiming to get away once every seven or ten days. Of course, if you're really committed to stress management, you can take shorter breaks every day--meditate for fifteen minutes, or spend some quiet time by yourself for half an hour before bed. Again, whatever works for you. My last suggestion is to keep a stress journal. Keep a little notebook with you, and write down a few notes when you're feeling stressed. What caused you to stress out? Work? Your kids? Balancing work and home life? Caring for your elderly parents? Health issues? Then, write down some of your symptoms so you can recognize them later. Are you irritable? Do your hands get shaky? Are you tired all the time? Is your heart racing? You might get symptoms that are unique to you—for example, I know a woman whose eyelid twitches when she gets really stressed. Sounds awfully weird, but it serves as a really good indicator to her. Finally, write down the steps you take to deal with the stress and whether they're successful or not so that you can review the things you've tried to see what works. This sounds like a lot of information, but it can be something short and sweet, like this:

04/16/13

—Stressed about work. Boss is asking too much, but I can't say no.

—Crabby all day at work. Snapped at Carol. Drinking way too much coffee.

—Went for a 15-minute walk over lunch. Feel a bit better.

04/21/13

—Told boss "no" when asked if I could take on another project. Wasn't easy, but should help.

## 6.3. Dietary Supplements

I get a lot of questions about dietary supplements, so I'll address them here. People often wonder if they should be taking multi-vitamins, or glucosamine, or chondroitin, or any number of other supplements that are popular. The first piece of advice that I can offer is to ask your doctor or another medical professional, as they can talk to you about your diet, whereas, without having met you, I can only make some general remarks. This is especially true if you're having symptoms that don't seem to be treated by the cleanse and subsequent diet. However, I can make a couple suggestions here.

First, take a multi-vitamin during the cleanse. Because you're cutting out a lot of foods, and you're not used to it, and you might not be sure of which foods have the correct micronutrients, it's a good idea to supplement with vitamins and minerals. Some of these are important in helping your body remove toxins, and the cleanse aims to help you be as efficient in that as possible, so a multi-vitamin can help. Once the cleanse is over, you may not need to take it anymore. It doesn't hurt to keep taking one, but if you use a highly detailed food log, you can get an idea of the amount of vitamins and minerals that you're getting and see whether you should be supplementing.

Second, consider taking an omega-3 supplement. Even though omega-3 is a long-chain triglyceride, it's one that's very good for you. As I discussed earlier, it's a crucial substance that helps keep your inflammatory system in check, so supplementing with this can give you a definite health boost . When I talk to people about this, I'm always careful to note that I prefer to get omega-3 from natural sources when at all possible, and so adding chia, oily fish, and omega-3-enhanced eggs is better than taking a supplement. Some people would rather just take a spoonful of fish oil every morning, though, and I can understand that. So, if you're one of those people (if you really hate eating fish, for example), you can supplement with one of these.

As I mentioned before, talk to your doctor. It's really the best way to go here. Also, if you're going to be taking a supplement, I recommend buying one from a health food store instead of from your neighborhood grocery store, as they're generally of higher quality and will be better absorbed by your body. They're more expensive, but think of it as an investment in your health.

## 6.4. Putting It All Together (and Keeping It Up)

Now that you know the principles behind the coconut oil diet, it's time to put it all together. You might be asking, "What do you mean put it all together? Don't I just . . . do it?" In a way, yes. But before I give you the recipes that will help make this diet a success, I want to make sure you understand that weight loss, no matter how you're going about it, requires more than just a rebalancing of your calorie intake and exercise. Losing weight is about making changes to your lifestyle—not just to your eating, and not just to your exercise, but also to the way you think about your daily life. Once you start losing weight, it'll be easier to see what I mean. Leading a healthy life is about more than losing weight, too. Once you start slimming down and improving your fitness, you're likely to want to kick some old bad habits, as well. You might find that once you've committed to eating better, you'll want to quit smoking. Or go to the doctor more regularly. Or try to find natural remedies for conditions that you'd treated with medications before. This change in mindstate may affect you in any number of ways, and I'd like to encourage you to embrace it wholeheartedly.

# Conclusion

Now that you've made it through the introduction to coconut oil, the basics of weight loss, and the coconut oil weight loss plan, you're well-equipped to start burning fat in a healthy, efficient, and permanent manner. All you need to do now is to start doing it! I've included a number of recipes here to get you started, and you can find literally thousands more online with a simple search. And if you're interested in using coconut oil for some non-culinary things, there are loads of websites that will give you ideas on how to use it.

Finally, I'd like to encourage you to share what you've learned here. The damage done by the food industry to coconut oil's reputation is a tragedy, and the only way that we can repair it is by letting everyone know how great of a product it is, and encouraging them to starting using it in their own daily lives! Don't let the myths perpetuated by ill-informed groups keep affecting how we live our lives. So talk to your friends, your family, your online communities, and anyone else who might listen! Make sure they know that there's more to the story of coconut oil than it just being "high in fat." This is a wonderful resource that we have at our disposal, and it would be a shame to not take advantage of it and share it as much as we can!

# 73 Mouth-Watering Coconut Oil Recipes

## BREAKFAST

### 1. Cranberry Carrot Muffins

Servings: 7
Preparation time: 15 minutes
Cook time: 20 minutes
Ready in: 35 minutes

## Nutrition Facts

Serving Size 179 g

**Amount Per Serving**

**Calories** 374     Calories from Fat 210

|  | % Daily Value* |
|---|---|
| **Total Fat** 23.3g | 36% |
| Saturated Fat 8.4g | 42% |
| *Trans* Fat 0.0g | |
| **Cholesterol** 70mg | 23% |
| **Sodium** 474mg | 20% |
| **Total Carbohydrates** 74.1g | 25% |
| Dietary Fiber 7.1g | 28% |
| Sugars 6.5g | |
| **Protein** 8.4g | |

| Vitamin A 107% | • | Vitamin C 8% |
|---|---|---|
| Calcium 4% | • | Iron 6% |

**Nutrition Grade C-**

* Based on a 2000 calorie diet

## Ingredients

- 2 cups gluten-free all-purpose flour
- 1 1/4 cups stevia
- 2 teaspoons baking soda

61

- 1/4 teaspoon sea salt
- 2 teaspoons pumpkin pie spice
- 2 cups shredded carrots
- 1/2 cup dried cranberries
- 1 cup chopped pecans
- 1/3 cup unshelled sunflower seeds
- 1/4 cup chopped apple
- 1 ripe banana, mashed
- 3 eggs
- 1/4 cup coconut oil, melted
- 2 teaspoons pure vanilla extract

## Directions

1. **Preheat** oven to 350 degrees F (175 degrees C). Line 12 muffin cups with paper liners.
2. **Mix** together flour, stevia, baking soda, salt, and pumpkin pie spice in a large bowl. Stir in the carrots, dried cranberries, pecans, sunflower seeds, apple, and mashed banana.
3. **Beat** the eggs in another bowl. Add the coconut oil and vanilla, beat well to combine.
4. **Pour** the egg mixture into the flour mixture and stir until well blended. Scoop the batter into prepared muffin cups.
5. **Bake** for 20 minutes, or until a toothpick inserted into center of a muffin comes out clean or with only a few crumbs sticking to it.

## 2. Maple Oat Granola

Servings: 6

Preparation time: 20 minutes

Cook time: 1 hour and 15 minutes

Ready in: 1 hour and 35 minutes

## Nutrition Facts

Serving Size 154 g

**Amount Per Serving**

**Calories** 548　　　　Calories from Fat 256

| | % Daily Value* |
|---|---:|
| **Total Fat** 28.4g | **44%** |
| Saturated Fat 12.8g | **64%** |
| Trans Fat 0.0g | |
| **Cholesterol** 0mg | **0%** |
| **Sodium** 164mg | **7%** |
| **Total Carbohydrates** 72.5g | **24%** |
| Dietary Fiber 11.8g | **47%** |
| Sugars 21.1g | |
| **Protein** 14.4g | |

| | | |
|---|---|---|
| Vitamin A 5% | • | Vitamin C 3% |
| Calcium 12% | • | Iron 26% |

**Nutrition Grade D+**

* Based on a 2000 calorie diet

## Ingredients

- 3 cups gluten-free rolled oats
- 1 cup blanched slivered almonds
- 1/3 cup ground flax seeds
- 1/2 cup unsweetened coconut flakes
- 1/3 cup unsalted sunflower seeds
- 1 tablespoon ground cinnamon
- 1/3 cup stevia
- 1/3 cup pure maple syrup
- 1/4 cup coconut oil, plus extra amount for greasing
- 2 teaspoons pure vanilla extract
- 2 tablespoons warm water
- 1/2 teaspoon sea salt
- 1/2 cup dried apricots

- 1/2 cup raisins

**Directions**

1. **Preheat** oven to 250 degrees F (120 degrees C). Grease a cookie sheet with coconut oil.
2. **Combine** the oats, almonds, ground flax seeds, coconut flakes, sunflower seeds, and cinnamon in a large bowl.
3. **Whisk** together the stevia, maple syrup, coconut oil, water and salt in another bowl until smooth.
4. **Pour** the maple syrup mixture over the oat mixture, and stir to coat. Spread mixture out on the prepared cookie sheet.
5. **Bake** for 1 hour and 15 minutes, stirring occasionally. Remove cookie sheet from oven then stir in dried apricots and raisins.
6. **Let** cool and serve.

# 3. Oatmeal Banana Pancakes

Servings: 4

Preparation time: 10 minutes

Cook time: 30 minutes

Ready in: 40 minutes

**Nutrition Facts**

Serving Size 219 g

**Amount Per Serving**

| | |
|---|---|
| **Calories** 476 | Calories from Fat 129 |

% Daily Value*

| | |
|---|---|
| **Total Fat** 14.4g | **22%** |
| Saturated Fat 9.2g | **46%** |
| *Trans* Fat 0.0g | |
| **Cholesterol** 0mg | **0%** |
| **Sodium** 302mg | **13%** |
| **Total Carbohydrates** 79.3g | **26%** |
| Dietary Fiber 7.1g | **28%** |
| Sugars 12.1g | |
| **Protein** 10.5g | |

| | |
|---|---|
| Vitamin A 2% | Vitamin C 13% |
| Calcium 8% | Iron 11% |

**Nutrition Grade D**

* Based on a 2000 calorie diet

## Ingredients

- 1 cup gluten-free quick cooking oats
- 1 cup gluten-free oat flour (or ground oats)
- 1/2 teaspoon gluten-free baking powder
- 1/2 teaspoon sea salt
- 1 teaspoon ground cinnamon
- 1/3 cup raw agave syrup
- 1/4 cup skim milk
- 3 egg whites
- 3 tablespoons melted coconut oil, plus extra amount for greasing
- 1 teaspoon pure vanilla extract
- 1 cup mashed ripe banana

## Directions

1. **Combine** the oats, oat flour, baking powder, salt, and cinnamon in a large bowl.
2. **Whisk** together the agave syrup, milk, egg whites, coconut oil, vanilla, and mashed banana in another bowl.
3. **Pour** the egg mixture into the oat mixture and stir well to combine.
4. **Grease** a pan or griddle with coconut oil then place over medium-high heat.
5. **Drop** batter (about 3 tablespoons per pancake) onto the griddle.
6. **Cook** each side for 2 to 3 minutes, until evenly browned. Repeat with the remaining batter.

## 4. Homemade Breakfast Cereal

Servings: 11
Preparation time: 15 minutes
Cook time: 1 hour
Ready in: 1 hour and 15 minutes

# Nutrition Facts

Serving Size 148 g

**Amount Per Serving**

**Calories** 476 — Calories from Fat 194

| | % Daily Value* |
|---|---|
| **Total Fat** 21.5g | **33%** |
| Saturated Fat 6.5g | **33%** |
| *Trans* Fat 0.0g | |
| **Cholesterol** 0mg | **0%** |
| **Sodium** 241mg | **10%** |
| **Total Carbohydrates** 70.4g | **23%** |
| Dietary Fiber 7.7g | **31%** |
| Sugars 16.2g | |
| **Protein** 13.2g | |

| | | |
|---|---|---|
| Vitamin A 0% | • | Vitamin C 3% |
| Calcium 5% | • | Iron 22% |

**Nutrition Grade C-**

* Based on a 2000 calorie diet

## Ingredients

- 7 cups quick cooking oats
- 2 cups oat bran

- 1/2 cup stevia
- 1/4 cup coconut oil, melted
- 1/4 cup applesauce
- 1/2 cup raw honey
- 1/2 cup water
- 1 tablespoon pure vanilla extract
- 2 teaspoon pumpkin pie spice
- 1 teaspoon sea salt
- 1 cup chopped dried cranberries
- 1 cup toasted chopped cashews
- 1 cup chopped pecans

## Directions

1. **Preheat** oven to 275 degrees F (135 degrees C).
2. **Mix** oats and oat bran in a large bowl.
3. **Blend** stevia, coconut oil, applesauce, honey, water, vanilla, pumpkin pie spice, and salt in a medium bowl.
4. **Pour** the coconut oil mixture into the oat mixture and stir until evenly moist. Spread mixture onto a large, shallow baking dish.
5. **Bake** 45 minutes, stirring often until lightly brown.
6. **Remove** dish from oven. Mix in dried cranberries, cashews, and pecans; continue baking for 15 minutes.
7. **Let** cool, and store in airtight containers.

## 5. Coconut Oatmeal with Walnuts and Dried Fruits

Servings: 5

Preparation time: 10 minutes

Cook time: 5 minutes

Ready in: 15 minutes

**Nutrition Facts**

Serving Size 317 g

**Amount Per Serving**

| | |
|---|---|
| **Calories** 454 | Calories from Fat 134 |

| | % Daily Value* |
|---|---|
| **Total Fat** 14.8g | **23%** |
| Saturated Fat 6.7g | **33%** |
| *Trans* Fat 0.0g | |
| **Cholesterol** 17mg | **6%** |
| **Sodium** 204mg | **9%** |
| **Total Carbohydrates** 67.3g | **22%** |
| Dietary Fiber 5.1g | **20%** |
| Sugars 41.1g | |
| **Protein** 15.5g | |

| | | |
|---|---|---|
| Vitamin A 1% | • | Vitamin C 4% |
| Calcium 15% | • | Iron 12% |

**Nutrition Grade C**

* Based on a 2000 calorie diet

### Ingredients

- 3 1/2 cups 2% milk
- 1/4 teaspoon sea salt
- 2 cups rolled oats
- 1 teaspoon pure vanilla extract
- 3 tablespoons raw honey
- 1/3 cup dates
- 1/3 cup dried blueberries
- 1/3 cup chopped walnuts
- 1/3 cup unsweetened coconut flakes
- 1 cup plain yogurt
- 1/4 cup pure maple syrup

### Directions

1. **Combine** milk and salt into a saucepan over medium-high, and bring to a boil.
2. **Stir** in the oats, vanilla, honey, dates, and dried blueberries; return to a boil. Reduce heat to medium.
3. **Cook** for 5 minutes. Add the walnuts and coconut flakes, stir and simmer until thick.
4. **Ladle** oatmeal into serving bowls, and top with yogurt and maple syrup.

## 6. Spicy Turkey Breakfast Sausage

Servings: 2

Preparation time: 10 minutes

Cook time: 20 minutes

Ready in: 30 minutes

# Nutrition Facts

Serving Size 313 g

**Amount Per Serving**

**Calories** 477      Calories from Fat 270

| | % Daily Value* |
|---|---|
| **Total Fat** 30.0g | **46%** |
| Saturated Fat 16.8g | **84%** |
| **Cholesterol** 161mg | **54%** |
| **Sodium** 1110mg | **46%** |
| **Total Carbohydrates** 8.5g | **3%** |
| Dietary Fiber 1.8g | **7%** |
| Sugars 5.4g | |
| **Protein** 45.3g | |

| | | |
|---|---|---|
| Vitamin A 43% | • | Vitamin C 130% |
| Calcium 7% | • | Iron 24% |

**Nutrition Grade C-**

* Based on a 2000 calorie diet

### Ingredients

- 1 pound lean ground turkey
- 1 red bell pepper, seeded and chopped
- 1 1/2 teaspoons ground sage
- 1/4 teaspoon of ground ginger
- 1/4 cup chopped fresh basil

- 1 teaspoon raw honey
- 1 teaspoons sea salt
- 1/2 teaspoon ground black pepper
- 2 cloves garlic, minced
- 1/4 teaspoon cayenne pepper
- 2 tablespoons coconut oil

**Directions**

1. **Combine** all ingredients, except for the coconut oil, in a large bowl.
2. **Shape** the mixture into 1/2-inch thick patties.
3. **Heat** the coconut oil in a skillet over medium heat.
4. **Add** patties and fry each side for 2 to 5 minutes, or until no longer pink inside and browned on both sides.

# 7. Eggplant and Mushroom Omelet

Servings: 5

Preparation time: 10 minutes

Cook time: 10 minutes

Ready in: 20 minutes

**Nutrition Facts**

Serving Size 398 g

**Amount Per Serving**

| | |
|---|---|
| **Calories** 418 | Calories from Fat 248 |

| | % Daily Value* |
|---|---|
| **Total Fat** 27.5g | **42%** |
| Saturated Fat 12.8g | **64%** |
| *Trans* Fat 0.0g | |
| **Cholesterol** 180mg | **60%** |
| **Sodium** 1264mg | **53%** |
| **Total Carbohydrates** 15.2g | **5%** |
| Dietary Fiber 6.7g | **27%** |
| Sugars 8.0g | |
| **Protein** 30.2g | |

| | | |
|---|---|---|
| Vitamin A 36% | • | Vitamin C 122% |
| Calcium 25% | • | Iron 28% |

**Nutrition Grade B-**

* Based on a 2000 calorie diet

## Ingredients

- 2 tablespoons melted coconut oil
- 4 medium sized Portobello mushrooms, trimmed and sliced
- 2 medium sized Eggplant, peeled and diced
- 1 cup red tomatoes, diced
- 2 green bell peppers, seeded and diced
- 2 eggs
- 1/2 teaspoon sea salt
- 1/4 teaspoon ground black pepper
- 1/2 cup finely chopped cilantro
- 1 cup shredded low-fat Parmesan cheese

**Directions**

1. **Heat** 1 tablespoon coconut oil in a medium skillet over medium heat. Add mushrooms, eggplant, tomatoes, and bell peppers; sauté for 4-5 minutes until just tender.
2. **Season** vegetables with 1/4 teaspoon of salt and a pinch of pepper. Transfer to a bowl, mix with 1/2 cup of cheese and set aside.
3. **Beat** the eggs in a separate bowl with remaining salt and pepper.
4. **Heat** remaining coconut oil in the skillet over medium heat. Add the egg mixture and cook for 2 minutes, or until set.
5. **Spoon** quarter of the vegetable mixture into the center of the omelet. Sprinkle remaining cheese and cilantro on top.
6. **Gently** fold one edge of the omelet over the vegetables using a spatula. Cover and cook for 2 more minutes or until cheese is melted. Transfer the omelet onto a plate and serve.

## 8. Coconut Banana Brownies

Servings: 4

Preparation time: 15 minutes

Cook time: 20 minutes

Ready in: 35 minutes

**Nutrition Facts**

Serving Size 171 g

Amount Per Serving

| | |
|---|---|
| **Calories** 413 | Calories from Fat 161 |

% Daily Value*

| | |
|---|---|
| **Total Fat** 17.9g | **28%** |
| Saturated Fat 5.8g | **29%** |
| *Trans* Fat 0.0g | |
| **Cholesterol** 44mg | **15%** |
| **Sodium** 227mg | **9%** |
| **Total Carbohydrates** 71.8g | **24%** |
| Dietary Fiber 20.5g | **82%** |
| Sugars 4.4g | |
| **Protein** 18.6g | |

| | | |
|---|---|---|
| Vitamin A 2% | • | Vitamin C 5% |
| Calcium 15% | • | Iron 25% |

**Nutrition Grade C**

* Based on a 2000 calorie diet

## Ingredients

- 1 1/2 cups gluten-free quick-cooking oats
- 1/2 cup stevia
- 1/2 cup unsweetened cocoa powder
- 3/4 cup flax seed meal
- 1/2 cup gluten-free all-purpose baking flour
- 1 teaspoon gluten-free baking powder
- 1/2 teaspoon ground cinnamon
- 1/4 teaspoon sea salt
- 1 omega-3 egg
- 1 ripe banana, mashed
- 1/4 cup coconut milk
- 1 teaspoon pure vanilla extract
- coconut oil for greasing

## Directions

1. **Preheat** oven to 350 degrees F (175 degrees C). Lightly grease an 8x10-inch baking pan with coconut oil.
2. **Combine** the oats, stevia, cocoa powder, flax seed meal, flour, baking powder, cinnamon, and salt in a bowl.
3. **Whisk** together the egg, mashed banana, coconut milk, and vanilla in a separate bowl.
4. **Pour** egg mixture into the flour mixture and stir to combine. Transfer batter to the prepared baking pan.
5. **Bake** for 20 minutes, or until a toothpick inserted in the center comes out clean or with only a few crumbs sticking to it.
6. **Let** cool, and slice brownies to serve.

## 9. Cheesy Baby Spinach Omelet

Servings: 2
Preparation time: 10 minutes
Cook time: 8 minutes
Ready in: 18 minutes

# Nutrition Facts

Serving Size 349 g

**Amount Per Serving**

**Calories** 397 — Calories from Fat 250

| | % Daily Value* |
|---|---|
| **Total Fat** 27.8g | **43%** |
| Saturated Fat 18.2g | **91%** |
| *Trans* Fat 0.0g | |
| **Cholesterol** 343mg | **114%** |
| **Sodium** 772mg | **32%** |
| **Total Carbohydrates** 16.9g | **6%** |
| Dietary Fiber 3.4g | **14%** |
| Sugars 7.0g | |
| **Protein** 22.0g | |

| | | |
|---|---|---|
| Vitamin A 53% | • | Vitamin C 24% |
| Calcium 28% | • | Iron 16% |

**Nutrition Grade B**

* Based on a 2000 calorie diet

## Ingredients

- 4 eggs

- 1/4 cup coconut milk
- 1/2 cup grated mozzarella cheese
- 1/2 teaspoon ground nutmeg
- 1/2 teaspoon sea salt
- 1/4 teaspoon ground black pepper
- 2 medium onions, chopped
- 1/4 cup unsweetened coconut flakes
- 1 1/2 cups torn baby spinach leaves
- 1 cup red tomatoes, diced
- coconut oil for greasing

## Directions

1. **Beat** together the eggs, coconut milk, cheese, nutmeg, salt, and pepper in a bowl.
2. **Stir** in the onions, coconut flakes, spinach, and tomatoes.
3. **Lightly** grease a small skillet with coconut oil. Place skillet over medium heat.
4. **Add** the egg mixture and cook on each side for about 3 minutes, or until set.

## 10. Pineapple Waffles with Macadamia and Coconut

Servings: 4

Preparation time: 15 minutes

Cook time: 10 minutes

Ready in: 25 minutes

## Nutrition Facts

Serving Size 212 g

**Amount Per Serving**

| | |
|---|---|
| **Calories** 505 | Calories from Fat 297 |

| | % Daily Value* |
|---|---|
| **Total Fat** 33.0g | **51%** |
| Saturated Fat 11.8g | **59%** |
| **Cholesterol** 56mg | **19%** |
| **Sodium** 418mg | **17%** |
| **Total Carbohydrates** 45.2g | **15%** |
| Dietary Fiber 6.9g | **28%** |
| Sugars 12.4g | |
| **Protein** 13.6g | |

| | | |
|---|---|---|
| Vitamin A 2% | • | Vitamin C 25% |
| Calcium 19% | • | Iron 8% |

**Nutrition Grade C+**

* Based on a 2000 calorie diet

## Ingredients

- 1 1/4 cups sifted gluten-free all-purpose flour
- 1 teaspoon gluten-free baking powder
- 1/4 teaspoon baking soda
- 1/4 teaspoon sea salt
- 1 cup plain yogurt
- 1 egg yolk
- 1/2 tablespoon raw honey
- 5 tablespoons low-fat unsalted butter, melted
- 1/4 cup coconut milk
- 3/4 cup chopped fresh pineapple
- 2 large egg whites, beaten
- 3/4 cup macadamia nuts, coarsely chopped
- coconut oil for greasing

## Directions

1. **Grease** a waffle iron with coconut oil then preheat.
2. **Combine** the flour, baking powder, baking soda, and salt in a medium bowl.
3. **Whisk** together the yogurt, egg yolk, honey, butter, coconut milk, and pineapple. Pour the yogurt mixture into flour mixture. Mix well and fold in egg whites and macadamia nuts.
4. **Pour** the mixture into the prepared waffle iron, and cook until golden brown.

## 11. Apple Carrot Muffins

Servings: 7

Preparation time: 15 minutes

Cook time: 20 minutes

Ready in: 35 minutes

# Nutrition Facts

Serving Size 187 g

**Amount Per Serving**

**Calories** 393      Calories from Fat 227

| | % Daily Value* |
|---|---|
| **Total Fat** 25.2g | **39%** |
| Saturated Fat 20.0g | **100%** |
| *Trans* Fat 0.0g | |
| **Cholesterol** 47mg | **16%** |
| **Sodium** 261mg | **11%** |
| **Total Carbohydrates** 77.8g | **26%** |
| Dietary Fiber 5.6g | **22%** |
| Sugars 7.0g | |
| **Protein** 7.2g | |

| | | |
|---|---|---|
| Vitamin A 89% | • | Vitamin C 5% |
| Calcium 11% | • | Iron 4% |

**Nutrition Grade C-**

* Based on a 2000 calorie diet

## Ingredients

- 2 1/4 cups gluten-free all-purpose flour
- 1 tablespoon gluten-free baking powder
- 1 tablespoon pumpkin pie spice

- 1/4 teaspoon sea salt
- 1 1/2 cup stevia
- 1 cup unsweetened coconut flakes
- 2 eggs
- 1/2 cup low-fat buttermilk
- 1/2 cup coconut oil, melted
- 3 carrots, grated
- 1 cup crushed apple

### Directions
1. **Preheat** oven to 375 degrees F (190 degrees C). Line 2 muffin pans with paper liners.
2. **Combine** the flour, baking powder, pumpkin pie spice, salt, stevia, and coconut flakes in a large bowl. In another bowl, whisk together the eggs, buttermilk, and coconut oil. Fold in the carrots and apple.
3. **Pour** the egg mixture into the flour mixture and mix until batter is moistened.
4. **Fill** each muffin cup with batter 3/4 full.
5. **Bake** for 20 minutes, or until a toothpick inserted into the center comes out clean.
6. **Let** cool and serve.

## 12. Banana Raspberry Bread with Almonds

Servings: 5
Preparation time: 15 minutes
Cook time: 1 hour
Ready in: 1 hour and 15 minutes

# Nutrition Facts

Serving Size 216 g

**Amount Per Serving**

**Calories** 361        Calories from Fat 167

% Daily Value*

| | |
|---|---|
| **Total Fat** 18.6g | **29%** |
| Saturated Fat 4.9g | **25%** |
| *Trans* Fat 0.0g | |
| **Cholesterol** 33mg | **11%** |
| **Sodium** 375mg | **16%** |
| **Total Carbohydrates** 66.3g | **22%** |
| Dietary Fiber 6.4g | **26%** |
| Sugars 16.8g | |
| **Protein** 18.7g | |

Vitamin A 2%    •    Vitamin C 24%
Calcium 17%    •    Iron 20%

**Nutrition Grade D+**

* Based on a 2000 calorie diet

## Ingredients

- 1 egg, beaten
- 4 ripe bananas, smashed
- 1/3 cup low-fat butter, melted
- 3/4 cup stevia
- 1 teaspoon pure coconut extract
- 1 teaspoon baking soda
- 1 pinch sea salt
- 1 1/2 cups gluten-free almond flour
- 1 cup raspberries, diced
- 1/2 cup chopped toasted sliced almonds
- coconut oil for greasing

## Directions

1. **Preheat** the oven to 350 degrees F (175 degrees C). Grease a 4x8 inch loaf pan with coconut oil.
2. **Whisk** together the egg, mashed bananas, and butter in a large mixing bowl.

3. **Add** the stevia, coconut extract, baking soda, and salt and mix well. Mix in the flour then fold in the raspberries and almonds. Pour mixture into the prepared loaf pan.
4. **Bake** for 1 hour.
5. **Let** cool and slice to serve.

## 13. Strawberry Mango Smoothie

Servings: 3

Ready in: 8 minutes

# Nutrition Facts

Serving Size 346 g

**Amount Per Serving**

**Calories** 443        Calories from Fat 254

| | % Daily Value* |
|---|---|
| **Total Fat** 28.2g | **43%** |
| Saturated Fat 21.6g | **108%** |
| *Trans* Fat 0.0g | |
| **Cholesterol** 0mg | **0%** |
| **Sodium** 26mg | **1%** |
| **Total Carbohydrates** 25.1g | **8%** |
| Dietary Fiber 11.9g | **48%** |
| Sugars 20.7g | |
| **Protein** 6.2g | |

| | | |
|---|---|---|
| Vitamin A 11% | • | Vitamin C 107% |
| Calcium 6% | • | Iron 14% |

**Nutrition Grade B-**

* Based on a 2000 calorie diet

## Ingredients

- 1 cup coconut milk
- 1/2 cup fresh lemon juice
- 2 frozen bananas, peeled and chopped
- 1/4 cup flax seed
- 2 teaspoons raw honey
- 1 cup frozen strawberries
- 1 mango, peeled, seeded, and diced
- 1 tablespoon coconut oil, melted

## Directions

1. **Place** all ingredients in a blender and blend until smooth.
2. **Chill,** pour into glasses and serve.

## 14. Coco Pumpkin Bread

Servings: 10

Preparation time: 15 minutes

Cook time: 1 hour

Ready in: 1 hour and 15 minutes

# Nutrition Facts

Serving Size 193 g

**Amount Per Serving**

| | |
|---|---|
| **Calories** 400 | Calories from Fat 221 |

**% Daily Value***

| | |
|---|---|
| **Total Fat** 24.5g | **38%** |
| Saturated Fat 12.9g | **65%** |
| *Trans* Fat 0.0g | |
| **Cholesterol** 65mg | **22%** |
| **Sodium** 656mg | **27%** |
| **Total Carbohydrates** 66.5g | **22%** |
| Dietary Fiber 7.7g | **31%** |
| Sugars 5.0g | |
| **Protein** 10.6g | |

| | | |
|---|---|---|
| Vitamin A 135% | • | Vitamin C 5% |
| Calcium 4% | • | Iron 15% |

**Nutrition Grade C+**

* Based on a 2000 calorie diet

## Ingredients

- 4 eggs
- 1/2 cup melted coconut oil, plus extra amount for greasing
- 1/2 cup applesauce
- 1 1/2 cups stevia
- 1 3/4 cup fresh pumpkin puree
- 3 1/2 cups gluten-free all-purpose flour
- 2 teaspoons baking soda
- 2 teaspoons sea salt
- 3 tablespoons pumpkin pie spice

- 2/3 cup water
- 1 cup unsweetened coconut flakes
- 1 cup chopped walnuts

**Directions**

1. **Preheat** oven to 350 degrees F (175 degrees C). Grease two 9 x 5 inch loaf pans with coconut oil.
2. **Whisk** together the eggs, coconut oil, applesauce, stevia, and pumpkin puree in a large mixing bowl.
3. **Add** flour, baking soda, salt, pumpkin pie spice, and water; whisk well until just moistened.
4. **Fold** in coconut flakes and walnuts. Pour batter into the prepared pans.
5. **Bake** for 1 hour, or until toothpick inserted in the center comes out clean.

## 15. Honey-Cinnamon Glazed Chocolate Donuts

Servings: 6

Preparation time: 15 minutes

Cook time: 10 minutes

Ready in: 25 minutes

## Nutrition Facts

Serving Size 160 g

**Amount Per Serving**

| | |
|---|---|
| **Calories** 408 | Calories from Fat 219 |

| | % Daily Value* |
|---|---|
| **Total Fat** 24.3g | **37%** |
| Saturated Fat 18.4g | **92%** |
| *Trans* Fat 0.0g | |
| **Cholesterol** 55mg | **18%** |
| **Sodium** 467mg | **19%** |
| **Total Carbohydrates** 73.5g | **25%** |
| Dietary Fiber 10.4g | **42%** |
| Sugars 9.1g | |
| **Protein** 9.0g | |

| | | |
|---|---|---|
| Vitamin A 2% | • | Vitamin C 2% |
| Calcium 10% | • | Iron 13% |

**Nutrition Grade D+**

* Based on a 2000 calorie diet

## Ingredients

- 2 cups gluten-free all-purpose flour
- 3/4 cup stevia
- 1/2 cup unsweetened cocoa powder
- 1 1/2 teaspoon instant coffee powder
- 1 teaspoon gluten-free baking powder
- 1 teaspoon baking soda
- 1/2 teaspoon sea salt
- 2 eggs
- 1 cup coconut milk
- 2 tablespoons unsalted low-fat butter, melted
- 2 teaspoons ground cinnamon
- 1 teaspoon pure vanilla extract
- coconut oil for greasing

*Honey-Cinnamon Glaze:*

- 1/4 cup ground cinnamon
- 1/4 cup coconut oil, softened
- 2 tablespoons raw honey, softened
- 2 teaspoons pure vanilla extract

**Directions**

1. **Preheat** the oven to 325 degrees F. Grease two 6-cavity donut pans with coconut oil.
2. **Combine** the flour, stevia, cocoa powder, coffee powder, baking powder, baking soda, and salt in a large bowl.
3. **Beat** together the eggs, coconut milk, butter, cinnamon, and vanilla until combined.
4. **Scoop** the batter into each donut cavity about 2/3 full.
5. **Bake** for 10 minutes. Cool donuts slightly on a wire rack.
6. **Place** all the glaze ingredients in a medium bowl. Set the bowl over hot water for 30 seconds and whisk the glaze mixture, until creamy.
7. **Spread** the glaze over the top of the donuts using a butter knife.

## 16. Vanilla Crepes with Apple Filling

Servings: 6

Preparation time: 15 minutes

Cook time: 15 minutes

Ready in: 30 minutes

**Nutrition Facts**

Serving Size 266 g

Amount Per Serving

Calories 434 — Calories from Fat 260

% Daily Value*

Total Fat 28.9g — 44%

Saturated Fat 19.4g — 97%

Trans Fat 0.0g

Cholesterol 105mg — 35%

Sodium 332mg — 14%

Total Carbohydrates 35.9g — 12%

Dietary Fiber 5.5g — 22%

Sugars 28.2g

Protein 5.7g

Vitamin A 4% • Vitamin C 14%

Calcium 5% • Iron 10%

Nutrition Grade D-

* Based on a 2000 calorie diet

### Ingredients

- 1 1/2 cups almond flour
- 2 teaspoons ground cinnamon
- 1 teaspoon ground nutmeg
- 1/2 teaspoon sea salt
- 3 egg yolks
- 1 1/2 cups coconut milk
- 2 tablespoons pure vanilla extract
- 2 tablespoons raw honey
- 5 tablespoons low-fat butter, melted
- coconut oil for greasing

*Apple Filling:*

- 3 tablespoons low-fat butter
- 4 granny smith apples, peeled cored and sliced thinly
- 2 tablespoons raw honey

- 1/4 cup pure vanilla extract
- 2 teaspoons fresh lemon juice
- 1/4 teaspoon sea salt

## Directions

1. **Combine** the flour, cinnamon, nutmeg, and salt in a large bowl.
2. **Beat** together the egg yolks, milk, vanilla, and honey in another bowl.
3. **Pour** egg mixture into the flour mixture and mix well until combined. Fold in the butter.
4. **Grease** a crepe pan with coconut oil then place over medium heat.
5. **Pour** batter (about 1/4 cup for every crepe) into the pan and tip to spread the batter thinly to the edges. Cook until golden brown on both sides.
6. **Prepare** the Apple Filling: Heat butter in a small saucepan over medium heat. Add the apples, honey, vanilla, lemon juice, and salt. Cook until the apples are soft.
7. **Cool** and stuff in crepes.

# 17. Cherry Chocolate Breakfast Cookies

Servings: 9

Preparation time: 12 minutes

Cook time: 10 minutes

Ready in: 22 minutes

## Nutrition Facts

Serving Size 114 g

**Amount Per Serving**

| | |
|---|---|
| **Calories** 477 | Calories from Fat 265 |

**% Daily Value\***

| | |
|---|---|
| **Total Fat** 29.5g | **45%** |
| Saturated Fat 8.8g | **44%** |
| *Trans* Fat 0.0g | |
| **Cholesterol** 36mg | **12%** |
| **Sodium** 403mg | **17%** |
| **Total Carbohydrates** 52.3g | **17%** |
| Dietary Fiber 6.5g | **26%** |
| Sugars 9.4g | |
| **Protein** 13.7g | |

| | | |
|---|---|---|
| Vitamin A 1% | • | Vitamin C 1% |
| Calcium 4% | • | Iron 11% |

**Nutrition Grade D**

\* Based on a 2000 calorie diet

## Ingredients

- 1 1/2 cups gluten-free old-fashioned rolled oats
- 1/3 cup coconut flour
- 1 cup ground walnuts
- 1/2 cup flax meal
- 1 teaspoon baking soda
- 1/2 teaspoon sea salt
- 1 teaspoon ground cinnamon
- 2 eggs
- 1/2 cup peanut butter
- 1/4 cup coconut oil, melted
- 1/4 cup raw honey
- 1/3 cup stevia
- 1 teaspoon pure vanilla extract
- 1/2 cup dried cherries

- 1 cup milk chocolate chips

**Directions**
1. **Preheat** oven to 375 degrees F (190 degrees C). Line baking sheets with parchment paper.
2. **Combine** the rolled oats, coconut flour, ground walnuts, flax meal, baking soda, salt, and cinnamon in a large mixing bowl.
3. **Whisk** together the eggs, peanut butter, coconut oil, honey, stevia, and vanilla in a separate bowl.
4. **Pour** the egg mixture into the flour mixture mix well to combine. Fold in the dried cherries and chocolate chips.
5. **Fill** a cookie scoop or tablespoon with dough then shape into balls. Drop the dough balls onto the prepared baking sheets, placing about 2 inches apart.
6. **Bake** 8 to 10 minutes, or until lightly browned. Remove baking sheets from oven and flatten the cookies with a spatula.
7. **Let** cool slightly on the baking sheets then transfer to wire racks.

## 18. Vegetable Frittata with Bread Cubes

Servings: 8

Preparation time: 15 minutes

Cook time: 1 hour

Ready in: 1 hour and 15 minutes

**Nutrition Facts**

Serving Size 205 g

**Amount Per Serving**

| | |
|---|---|
| **Calories** 382 | Calories from Fat 274 |

| | % Daily Value* |
|---|---|
| **Total Fat** 30.5g | **47%** |
| Saturated Fat 18.6g | **93%** |
| Trans Fat 0.0g | |
| **Cholesterol** 190mg | **63%** |
| **Sodium** 627mg | **26%** |
| **Total Carbohydrates** 16.5g | **6%** |
| Dietary Fiber 3.8g | **15%** |
| Sugars 3.6g | |
| **Protein** 14.6g | |

| | | |
|---|---|---|
| Vitamin A 97% | • | Vitamin C 31% |
| Calcium 14% | • | Iron 11% |

**Nutrition Grade B**

* Based on a 2000 calorie diet

### Ingredients

- 3 tablespoons coconut oil, plus extra amount for greasing
- 1 1/2 cups chopped carrots
- 1 1/2 cups chopped fresh mushrooms
- 1/2 cup chopped red bell pepper
- 1/2 cup chopped green bell pepper
- 1/2 cup diced red tomatoes
- 3/4 cup chopped onion
- 3 cloves garlic, minced
- 6 eggs, beaten
- 2 cups fat-free cream cheese, diced
- 1/4 cup coconut cream
- 2 cups shredded Cheddar cheese
- 4 slices gluten-free bread, cubed
- 1 teaspoon sea salt

- 1/4 teaspoon ground black pepper

**Directions**

1. **Preheat** oven to 350 degrees F (175 degrees C). Lightly grease a 9x13 inch baking dish with coconut oil.
2. **Heat** 3 tablespoons coconut oil in a large skillet over medium high heat.
3. **Add** carrots, mushrooms, bell peppers, tomatoes, onion, and garlic, sauté until vegetables are tender. Remove skillet from heat and set aside.
4. **Beat** together the eggs, cream cheese, and coconut cream in a large bowl. Stir in the cheddar cheese, bread cubes and sautéed vegetables, salt, and pepper. Pour mixture into the prepared baking dish.
5. **Bake** for 1 hour, or until set. Serve warm.

## 19. Apple Quinoa Porridge

Servings: 5
Preparation time: 10 minutes
Cook time: 25 minutes
Ready in: 35 minutes

```
Nutrition Facts
Serving Size 276 g

Amount Per Serving
Calories 456              Calories from Fat 236
                               % Daily Value*
Total Fat 26.2g                          40%
  Saturated Fat 16.9g                    85%
  Trans Fat 0.0g
Cholesterol 0mg                           0%
Sodium 214mg                              9%
Total Carbohydrates 53.9g                18%
  Dietary Fiber 6.9g                     28%
  Sugars 24.7g
Protein 7.9g

Vitamin A 1%           •        Vitamin C 7%
Calcium 6%             •             Iron 18%

Nutrition Grade D
* Based on a 2000 calorie diet
```

**Ingredients**

- 1 cup red quinoa, rinsed and drained
- 2 cups water
- 1 tablespoon low-fat butter
- 1 apple, peeled, cored and diced
- 1/2 cup raisins
- 1/2 teaspoon sea salt
- 1 tablespoon ground cinnamon
- 2 teaspoons pure vanilla extract
- 2 tablespoons raw honey
- 1/3 cup sliced pecans
- 1 1/2 cups almond milk
- 1 tablespoon coconut cream

**Directions**

1. **Place** the quinoa and water in a saucepan over high heat then bring to a boil.

2. **Reduce** heat to medium-low. Simmer covered for 15 to 20 minutes until the quinoa is tender and the water has been absorbed.

3. **Melt** the butter in a large skillet over medium heat. Add the apple, raisins, salt, cinnamon, vanilla, and honey.

4. **Stir** in the pecans and cook for 3 minutes, stirring until the apple is hot and beginning to soften.

5. **Pour** in the almond milk and coconut cream; simmer until hot.

6. **Add** the cooked quinoa, and cook for 5 minutes. Serve warm.

## 20. Chicken Quinoa Pilaf

Servings: 4

Preparation time: 15 minutes

Cook time: 35 minutes

Ready in: 50 minutes

# Nutrition Facts

Serving Size 273 g

**Amount Per Serving**

**Calories** 445　　　　Calories from Fat 237

| | % Daily Value* |
|---|---|
| **Total Fat** 26.4g | **41%** |
| Saturated Fat 19.6g | **98%** |
| *Trans* Fat 0.0g | |
| **Cholesterol** 31mg | **10%** |
| **Sodium** 329mg | **14%** |
| **Total Carbohydrates** 36.3g | **12%** |
| Dietary Fiber 6.3g | **25%** |
| Sugars 5.0g | |
| **Protein** 18.5g | |

| | | |
|---|---|---|
| Vitamin A 155% | • | Vitamin C 12% |
| Calcium 6% | • | Iron 22% |

**Nutrition Grade B**

* Based on a 2000 calorie diet

**Ingredients**

- 2 tablespoons coconut oil, melted
- 1 clove garlic, crushed and chopped
- 1 small onion, diced
- 3 carrots, diced
- 1 stalk celery, diced
- 1 cup quinoa
- 1 cup low-sodium chicken broth
- 1 cup light coconut milk
- 1 teaspoon dried basil
- 1 teaspoon dried cilantro
- 1 teaspoon dried rosemary
- 1 teaspoon chopped fresh marjoram
- 2 teaspoons chopped fresh mint
- 1 cup cooked chicken meat, shredded
- 1 teaspoon curry powder
- 1/2 teaspoon sea salt
- 1/4 teaspoon ground black pepper

## Directions

1. **Heat** the coconut oil in a saucepan over medium heat.
2. **Add** the garlic, onion, carrots, and celery, sauté in hot oil for about 7 minutes, or until tender.
3. **Stir** in the quinoa, chicken broth, coconut milk, and the herbs. Turn heat to high and bring mixture to a boil. Reduce heat to medium-low.
4. **Simmer** covered for 20 minutes, or until the quinoa is tender and the liquid has been absorbed.
5. **Stir** in the chicken, curry powder, salt, and pepper.

## 21. Banana Cake with Chocolate and Walnuts

Servings: 12

Preparation time: 15 minutes

Cook time: 30 minutes

Ready in: 45 minutes

## Nutrition Facts

Serving Size 147 g

**Amount Per Serving**

| | |
|---|---|
| **Calories** 423 | Calories from Fat 206 |

**% Daily Value\***

| | |
|---|---|
| **Total Fat** 22.8g | **35%** |
| Saturated Fat 11.7g | **58%** |
| Trans Fat 0.0g | |
| **Cholesterol** 28mg | **9%** |
| **Sodium** 381mg | **16%** |
| **Total Carbohydrates** 68.7g | **23%** |
| Dietary Fiber 6.8g | **27%** |
| Sugars 22.9g | |
| **Protein** 7.7g | |

| | |
|---|---|
| Vitamin A 1% | Vitamin C 2% |
| Calcium 4% | Iron 11% |

**Nutrition Grade D-**

\* Based on a 2000 calorie diet

## Ingredients

- 2 cups gluten-free all-purpose flour
- 1 cup quick cooking oats
- 1/4 cup milled flaxseed
- 1/4 cup natural cocoa powder
- 1 1/2 teaspoons baking soda
- 1 teaspoon sea salt
- 1/2 cup low-fat butter
- 1/2 cup fat-free vanilla yogurt
- 1 cup stevia
- 2 eggs
- 1/2 cup low-fat buttermilk
- 1 teaspoon pure vanilla extract
- 1 cup mashed bananas

94

- 1/2 cup chopped walnuts
- 1/2 cup unsweetened coconut flakes
- 2 cups semisweet chocolate chips
- coconut oil for greasing

**Directions**

1. **Preheat** oven to 350 degrees F (175 degrees C). Grease a 9x13 inch pan with coconut oil.
2. **Combine** the flour, oats, flaxseed, cocoa powder, baking soda, and salt in a medium bowl.
3. **Cream** together the butter, yogurt, and stevia until light and fluffy in a large bowl. Whisk in eggs one at a time.
4. **Mix** in buttermilk, vanilla, and bananas. Add the flour mixture and mix well to combine. Fold in the walnuts, coconut flakes, and chocolate chips. Transfer batter to the prepared pan.
5. **Bake** for 30 to 35 minutes, or until a toothpick inserted into the cake comes out clean or with only a few crumbs sticking to it.

# LUNCH

## 22. Sweet Potato Casserole

Servings: 7

Preparation time: 15 minutes

Cook time: 30 minutes

Ready in: 45 minutes

## Nutrition Facts

Serving Size 157 g

**Amount Per Serving**

**Calories** 346 | Calories from Fat 233

| | % Daily Value* |
|---|---|
| **Total Fat** 25.9g | **40%** |
| Saturated Fat 15.6g | **78%** |
| *Trans* Fat 0.0g | |
| **Cholesterol** 52mg | **17%** |
| **Sodium** 195mg | **8%** |
| **Total Carbohydrates** 51.5g | **17%** |
| Dietary Fiber 3.1g | **12%** |
| Sugars 3.4g | |
| **Protein** 8.5g | |

| | | |
|---|---|---|
| Vitamin A 4% | • | Vitamin C 14% |
| Calcium 8% | • | Iron 12% |

**Nutrition Grade C+**

* Based on a 2000 calorie diet

## Ingredients

- 2 cups sweet potatoes, peeled and mashed
- 1 cup stevia
- 2 eggs, beaten
- 1/2 cup low-fat butter, melted
- 1/2 cup evaporated milk
- 2 teaspoons pumpkin pie spice
- 1 cup unsweetened coconut flakes
- 3/4 cups gluten-free cornflakes cereal, crushed
- 1/4 cup oatmeal
- 1/2 cup chopped almonds
- 1/2 cup low-fat butter, melted

**Directions**

1. **Preheat** oven to 400 degrees F (200 degrees C). Grease a 9x13 inch baking dish with butter.

2. **Mix** together the mashed sweet potatoes, stevia, eggs, 1/2 cup butter, evaporated milk, pumpkin pie spice, and coconut flakes. Place mixture into the prepared baking dish.

3. **Bake** 20 minutes, or until sweet potatoes are tender.

4. **Combine** the crushed cornflakes, oatmeal, almonds, and remaining butter. Spread the topping over the baked casserole.

5. **Return** the casserole to the oven and bake for 10 minutes more.

# 23. Spicy Lentil Curry

Servings: 2

Preparation time: 10 minutes

Cook time: 30 minutes

Ready in: 40 minutes

## Nutrition Facts

Serving Size 320 g

**Amount Per Serving**

| Calories 522 | Calories from Fat 207 |
|---|---|
| | **% Daily Value*** |
| **Total Fat** 23.0g | **35%** |
| Saturated Fat 19.2g | **96%** |
| Trans Fat 0.0g | |
| **Cholesterol** 0mg | **0%** |
| **Sodium** 527mg | **22%** |
| **Total Carbohydrates** 69.2g | **23%** |
| Dietary Fiber 20.8g | **83%** |
| Sugars 25.8g | |
| **Protein** 17.5g | |

| Vitamin A 3% | • | Vitamin C 16% |
|---|---|---|
| Calcium 11% | • | Iron 44% |

**Nutrition Grade B**

* Based on a 2000 calorie diet

**Ingredients**

- 1/2 cup dried lentils, rinsed
- 1 cup low-sodium chicken broth
- 3/4 cup coconut cream
- 3/4 cup raisins
- 1 tablespoon curry powder
- 2 teaspoons dried coriander
- 2 teaspoons ground cinnamon
- 1 teaspoon dried cumin
- 1 teaspoon cardamom
- 1/2 teaspoon sea salt
- 1 jalapeno pepper, seeded and minced
- 1 thumb-size fresh ginger root, peeled and grated

## Directions

1. **Place** lentils and chicken broth in a saucepan over low heat.
2. **Bring** to a boil, and simmer covered for 15 minutes.
3. **Stir** in the coconut cream, raisins, curry powder, coriander, cinnamon, cumin, cardamom, and salt. Add the jalapeno pepper and ginger.
4. **Simmer** for 10 to 15 minutes more, or until tender.

## 24. Cabbage Coconut Curry

Servings: 3

Preparation time: 15 minutes

Cook time: 10 minutes

Ready in: 25 minutes

```
Nutrition Facts
Serving Size 454 g

Amount Per Serving
Calories 295              Calories from Fat 168
                              % Daily Value*
Total Fat 18.6g                        29%
   Saturated Fat 14.7g                 74%
   Trans Fat 0.0g
Cholesterol 0mg                         0%
Sodium 436mg                           18%
Total Carbohydrates 31.1g              10%
   Dietary Fiber 11.9g                 48%
   Sugars 15.4g
Protein 7.0g

Vitamin A 155%        •      Vitamin C 269%
Calcium 15%           •          Iron 20%
Nutrition Grade A-
* Based on a 2000 calorie diet
```

## Ingredients

- 1 tablespoon coconut oil, melted
- 2 tablespoons low-fat butter
- 1 clove garlic, minced
- 1 small yellow onion, thinly sliced
- 1 thumb-size fresh ginger root, peeled and grated
- 1 cup julienned carrots
- 1 small head cabbage, sliced
- 1 cup cauliflower florets
- 1/2 cup fresh shredded coconut
- 1 green bell pepper, diced
- 2 tablespoons Indian curry powder
- 3/4 cup coconut milk
- 1/2 teaspoon sea salt (or to taste)

- 1/4 teaspoon ground black pepper (or to taste)
- 1/4 cup granny smith apple, peeled and diced
- 1/4 cup chopped green onions

### Directions

1. **Heat** the coconut oil and butter in a large skillet over high heat.
2. **Add** the garlic, onion, ginger, and carrot, sauté for about 1 minute, until onion just starts to soften. Stir in the cabbage, cauliflower, coconut, bell pepper, and curry powder; cook for 2 more minutes.
3. **Reduce** heat to medium-low. Pour in the coconut milk, season with salt, and pepper; simmer until heated through.
4. **Stir** in apple and green onions.

## 25. Jamaican Beans and Brown Rice

Servings: 7
Preparation time: 10 minutes
Cook time: 2 hours 35 minutes
Ready in: 2 hours and 45 minutes

# Nutrition Facts

Serving Size 156 g

**Amount Per Serving**

**Calories** 425       Calories from Fat 93

| | % Daily Value* |
|---|---|
| **Total Fat** 10.3g | **16%** |
| Saturated Fat 7.7g | **38%** |
| **Cholesterol** 0mg | **0%** |
| **Sodium** 13mg | **1%** |
| **Total Carbohydrates** 71.8g | **24%** |
| Dietary Fiber 8.6g | **35%** |
| Sugars 2.9g | |
| **Protein** 13.2g | |

| | | |
|---|---|---|
| Vitamin A 2% | • | Vitamin C 25% |
| Calcium 7% | • | Iron 28% |

**Nutrition Grade B+**

* Based on a 2000 calorie diet

## Ingredients

- 1 1/4 cups dry kidney beans
- 1 cup coconut milk
- 1 teaspoon minced garlic
- 1 onion, finely chopped
- 2 tablespoons fresh thyme
- 1/2 teaspoon ground allspice
- 1 hot red chili pepper, sliced
- 2 1/4 cups uncooked brown rice
- 2 tablespoons chopped green onions
- 1 teaspoon grated fresh ginger
- 1 tablespoon freshly squeezed lime juice

## Directions

1. **Place** the beans and coconut milk in a large saucepan over low heat; cook for 2 hours.
2. **Stir** in garlic, onions, thyme, allspice, and chili pepper.
3. **Simmer** for 7 minutes. Stir in the rice, green onions, and ginger; bring to a boil.
4. **Reduce** heat, simmer covered for 25 minutes, or until all liquid is absorbed and rice is tender.
5. **Fluff** with a fork then drizzle with lime juice.

## 26. Coconut Lentil Stew over Quinoa

Servings: 7

Preparation time: 15 minutes

Cook time: 40 minutes

Ready in: 55 minutes

## Nutrition Facts

Serving Size 457 g

**Amount Per Serving**

**Calories** 614      Calories from Fat 219

| | % Daily Value* |
|---|---|
| **Total Fat** 24.4g | **37%** |
| Saturated Fat 17.0g | **85%** |
| **Cholesterol** 0mg | **0%** |
| **Sodium** 1136mg | **47%** |
| **Total Carbohydrates** 77.7g | **26%** |
| Dietary Fiber 23.9g | **96%** |
| Sugars 9.0g | |
| **Protein** 25.4g | |

Vitamin A 5%   •   Vitamin C 48%

Calcium 9%   •   Iron 58%

**Nutrition Grade A-**

* Based on a 2000 calorie diet

## Ingredients

- 2 cups quinoa, rinsed
- 3 1/2 cups low-sodium chicken broth
- 1 tablespoon sea salt
- 2 tablespoons coconut oil, melted
- 6 cloves garlic, minced
- 1 small onion, chopped
- 4 large tomatoes, chopped
- 1 cup water
- 1 3/4 cups coconut milk
- 1 tablespoon raw honey
- 1/4 cup coconut powder
- 3 tablespoons curry powder
- 2 1/2 tablespoons garam masala
- 2 cups red lentils

- 1 teaspoon sea salt (or to taste)
- 1/2 teaspoon ground black pepper
- 1 cup fresh cilantro, chopped
- 1/4 cup toasted cashews, coarsely chopped

**Directions**

1. **Boil** 3 1/2 cups of water and 1 tablespoon of salt in a saucepan over high heat. Add the quinoa then reduce the heat to medium-low.
2. **Cover** and simmer for about 15 minutes, or until the quinoa is tender and liquid is absorbed. Set aside, and keep warm.
3. **Heat** the coconut oil in a large saucepan over medium heat. Stir in the garlic and onion; sauté for 5 minutes or until the onion has softened. Add the tomatoes, and cook for additional 5 minutes. Turn heat to medium-high.
4. **Pour** in the water, coconut milk, honey, coconut powder, curry powder, and garam masala. Add the lentils, and simmer for 10 to 15 minutes, or until just tender; stirring frequently. Season stew with salt and pepper, and then sprinkle with the chopped cilantro.
5. **Serve** the lentil stew over quinoa.

## 27. Crock Pot Pork and Squash Stew

Servings: 5

Preparation time: 15 minutes

Cook time: 5 hours

Ready in: 5 hours and 15 minutes

**Nutrition Facts**

Serving Size 487 g

Amount Per Serving

Calories 559 — Calories from Fat 165

% Daily Value*

| | |
|---|---|
| **Total Fat** 18.3g | **28%** |
| Saturated Fat 7.6g | **38%** |
| *Trans* Fat 0.0g | |
| **Cholesterol** 209mg | **70%** |
| **Sodium** 924mg | **39%** |
| **Total Carbohydrates** 23.4g | **8%** |
| Dietary Fiber 6.0g | **24%** |
| Sugars 6.3g | |
| **Protein** 73.4g | |

Vitamin A 234% • Vitamin C 60%

Calcium 14% • Iron 29%

**Nutrition Grade A**

* Based on a 2000 calorie diet

### Ingredients

- 2 1/2 pounds pork loin chops, cubed
- 2 leeks, trimmed and sliced
- 4 celery stalks, chopped
- 2 shallots, diced
- 7 cloves garlic, thinly sliced
- 4 cups cubed butternut squash
- 1 medium carrot, sliced
- 1/2 cup diced tomatoes
- 1 teaspoon ground rosemary
- 1 teaspoon ground sage
- 1/2 teaspoon paprika
- 1 chili pepper, minced
- 2 teaspoons sea salt

- 1 1/2 teaspoons fresh squeezed lemon juice
- 1/4 cup coconut milk
- 1 cup low-sodium chicken broth

## Directions

1. **Combine** the pork and vegetables in a 4-quart slow cooker.
2. **Cover** with the spices, lemon juice, coconut milk, and chicken broth; mix well.
3. **Cook** for 5 hours on High, or 7 hours on Low.

## 28. Turkey Bean Chili

Servings: 7

Preparation time: 15 minutes

Cook time: 1 hour

Ready in: 1 hour and 15 minutes

## Nutrition Facts

Serving Size 340 g

**Amount Per Serving**

| | |
|---|---|
| **Calories** 498 | Calories from Fat 98 |

| | % Daily Value* |
|---|---|
| **Total Fat** 10.9g | **17%** |
| Saturated Fat 5.2g | **26%** |
| *Trans* Fat 0.0g | |
| **Cholesterol** 23mg | **8%** |
| **Sodium** 619mg | **26%** |
| **Total Carbohydrates** 74.2g | **25%** |
| Dietary Fiber 18.8g | **75%** |
| Sugars 14.6g | |
| **Protein** 29.9g | |

| | | |
|---|---|---|
| Vitamin A 75% | • | Vitamin C 54% |
| Calcium 18% | • | Iron 46% |

**Nutrition Grade A**

* Based on a 2000 calorie diet

## Ingredients

- 1/2 pound ground lean turkey
- 2 3/4 cups natural tomato soup
- 1 1/4 cups water

- 1 tablespoon garlic powder
- 1 onion, chopped
- 1 red bell pepper, minced
- 1 tablespoon grated fresh ginger
- 1 3/4 cup garbanzo beans, rinsed
- 1 3/4 cup red kidney beans, rinsed
- 1/2 medium sweet potato, peeled and cubed
- 1/2 cup chopped carrot
- 3 tablespoons curry powder
- 1 teaspoon sea salt (or to taste)
- 1/2 teaspoon ground black pepper (to taste)
- 1/4 cup mango jam
- 1/2 cup coconut milk, divided

**Directions**

1. **Place** the ground turkey in a large skillet over medium heat. Fry for 5 to 7 minutes until completely browned. Drain grease from the turkey.
2. **Mix** the tomato soup, water, and garlic powder in a large pot then bring to a boil. Add the cooked turkey and bring mixture to a boil. Reduce heat to medium-low.
3. **Stir** in the onion, bell pepper, ginger, beans, sweet potato, carrot, curry powder, salt, pepper, and mango jam. Cover, and simmer for about 15 minutes, or until the beans are tender.
4. **Add** the coconut milk and simmer for additional 40 minutes.

# 29. Creamy Chicken Noodle Soup

Servings: 4

Preparation time: 10 minutes

Cook time: 20 minutes

Ready in: 30 minutes

## Nutrition Facts

Serving Size 662 g

**Amount Per Serving**

**Calories** 500 — Calories from Fat 96

% Daily Value*

| | % Daily Value* |
|---|---|
| **Total Fat** 10.7g | **16%** |
| Saturated Fat 5.9g | **30%** |
| Trans Fat 0.0g | |
| **Cholesterol** 62mg | **21%** |
| **Sodium** 773mg | **32%** |
| **Total Carbohydrates** 70.5g | **24%** |
| Dietary Fiber 5.2g | **21%** |
| Sugars 2.3g | |
| **Protein** 30.0g | |

Vitamin A 89%  •  Vitamin C 50%
Calcium 9%  •  Iron 31%

**Nutrition Grade B**

* Based on a 2000 calorie diet

## Ingredients

- 10 ounce gluten-free dry flat Thai rice noodles
- 6 cups low-sodium pure chicken broth
- 2 cups chicken breasts, diced
- 1/2 cup mushrooms, diced
- 1 large carrot, sliced
- 1/4 cup ginger, grated
- 1 bay leaf
- 1 teaspoon fresh thyme, chopped
- 1/2 teaspoon red pepper flakes
- 2 cloves garlic, minced
- 3 tablespoons gluten-free soy sauce
- 1/2 teaspoon freshly ground black pepper
- 1/4 cup fresh lemon juice

- 1/3 cup coconut milk
- 1 teaspoon stevia
- 1 cup fresh parsley, chopped

## Directions

1. **Boil** the noodles in a large pot of lightly salted water according to package directions, or until al dente. Rinse with cold water, drain and set aside.
2. **Place** the chicken broth in a large pot over high heat and bring to a boil. Add the chicken, mushrooms, carrot, ginger, and bay leaf. Boil mixture for 1 minute over High heat. Reduce heat to medium. Cover pot and simmer for 5 minutes.
3. **Stir** in thyme, red pepper flakes, garlic, soy sauce, black pepper, and lemon juice.
4. **Reduce** heat to low then stir in the coconut milk and stevia. Place noodles in serving bowls then ladle the chicken soup over the top.
5. **Sprinkle** soup with chopped parsley and serve.

## 30. Spicy Cod Stew

Servings: 6

Preparation time: 30 minutes

Cook time: 25 minutes

Ready in: 55 minutes

## Nutrition Facts

Serving Size 415 g

**Amount Per Serving**

| | |
|---|---|
| **Calories** 385 | Calories from Fat 224 |

**% Daily Value***

| | |
|---|---|
| **Total Fat** 24.8g | **38%** |
| Saturated Fat 17.7g | **88%** |
| Trans Fat 0.0g | |
| **Cholesterol** 40mg | **13%** |
| **Sodium** 416mg | **17%** |
| **Total Carbohydrates** 19.3g | **6%** |
| Dietary Fiber 6.1g | **24%** |
| Sugars 10.4g | |
| **Protein** 24.4g | |

| | | |
|---|---|---|
| Vitamin A 84% | • | Vitamin C 278% |
| Calcium 4% | • | Iron 18% |

**Nutrition Grade B-**

* Based on a 2000 calorie diet

## Ingredients

- 1 1/2 pounds cod fillets, cut into chunks
- 3 cloves garlic, minced
- 3 tablespoons lime juice
- 1 tablespoon ground coriander
- 3/4 tablespoon cayenne pepper
- 1 teaspoon sea salt
- 1 teaspoon ground black pepper
- 2 tablespoons olive oil
- 2 onions, chopped
- 1 tablespoon chopped fresh ginger
- 4 large bell peppers, sliced
- 2 cups diced tomatoes
- 2 cups coconut milk
- 1/4 cup chopped green onions

110

- 1 bunch fresh parsley, chopped

**Directions**

1. **Place** cod chunks in a large mixing bowl.
2. **Mix** the garlic, lime juice, coriander, cayenne pepper, salt, and pepper in a small bowl. Pour mixture over cod and toss to coat.
3. **Cover** and refrigerate for at least 20 minutes, or overnight for best flavor.
4. **Heat** the olive oil in a large pot over medium-high heat.
5. **Add** the onions and sauté in oil for 1 minute. Reduce heat to medium. Stir in the ginger, bell peppers, tomatoes, and cod.
6. **Pour** in coconut milk, cover the pot, and simmer for 15 minutes, stirring occasionally.
7. **Stir** in the green onions and parsley and simmer for additional 5 to 10 minutes, or until the fish is cooked through.

## 31. Coconut Brown Rice and Black Beans

Servings: 6

Preparation time: 8 minutes

Cook time: 25 minutes

Ready in: 33 minutes

## Nutrition Facts

Serving Size 213 g

**Amount Per Serving**

**Calories** 483      Calories from Fat 124

| | % Daily Value* |
|---|---|
| **Total Fat** 13.8g | **21%** |
| Saturated Fat 9.2g | **46%** |
| **Cholesterol** 0mg | **0%** |
| **Sodium** 25mg | **1%** |
| **Total Carbohydrates** 73.4g | **24%** |
| Dietary Fiber 13.4g | **54%** |
| Sugars 3.8g | |
| **Protein** 19.3g | |

| | | |
|---|---|---|
| Vitamin A 2% | • | Vitamin C 8% |
| Calcium 11% | • | Iron 28% |

**Nutrition Grade B+**

* Based on a 2000 calorie diet

### Ingredients

- 1 tablespoon olive oil, melted
- 2 cloves garlic, chopped
- 1 red onion, minced
- 1 cup uncooked brown rice
- 1 cup coconut milk
- 1 cup low-sodium chicken broth
- 1/2 teaspoon turmeric
- 1 pinch chili powder
- 1 (15 ounce) can black beans, rinsed and drained
- 1/2 cup thinly sliced green onions

### Directions

1. **Heat** olive oil in a small saucepan over medium heat. Add the garlic and cook until lightly browned. Stir in

112

onion, and cook for about 3 minutes, or until soft and translucent.

2.  **Stir** in the rice and cook until coated with oil. Pour in the coconut milk and chicken broth; season with turmeric and chili powder.

3.  **Bring** mixture to a boil over high heat. Reduce heat to medium-low, cover, and simmer for about 18 minutes, or until the rice is tender and the liquid has been absorbed.

4.  **Add** the black beans and stir, and cook a few minutes until heated through. Sprinkle with green onions to serve.

## 32. Spicy Thai Coconut Soup

Servings: 8

Preparation time: 15 minutes

Cook time: 30 minutes

Ready in: 45 minutes

# Nutrition Facts

Serving Size 317 g

**Amount Per Serving**

**Calories** 369          Calories from Fat 279

| | % Daily Value* |
|---|---|
| **Total Fat** 31.0g | **48%** |
| Saturated Fat 25.7g | **129%** |
| *Trans* Fat 0.0g | |
| **Cholesterol** 89mg | **30%** |
| **Sodium** 719mg | **30%** |
| **Total Carbohydrates** 13.0g | **4%** |
| Dietary Fiber 3.7g | **15%** |
| Sugars 7.2g | |
| **Protein** 14.9g | |

| | | |
|---|---|---|
| Vitamin A 25% | • | Vitamin C 18% |
| Calcium 4% | • | Iron 26% |

**Nutrition Grade C+**

* Based on a 2000 calorie diet

## Ingredients

- 1 tablespoon olive oil
- 1 stalk lemon grass, minced
- 2 tablespoons grated fresh ginger

113

- 2 teaspoons red curry paste
- 4 cups low-sodium chicken broth
- 3 tablespoons fish sauce
- 1 tablespoon raw honey
- 5 cups light coconut milk
- 1 medium carrot, diced
- 1/2 pound fresh white mushrooms, sliced
- 1/2 cup green peas
- 1 pound medium shrimp, peeled and deveined
- 2 tablespoons fresh lime juice
- 1/2 teaspoon sea salt
- 1/4 cup chopped green onions
- 1/4 cup chopped fresh parsley

**Directions**

1. **Heat** the oil in a large pot over medium heat. Stir in the lemongrass, ginger, and curry paste and cook for 1 minute.
2. **Pour** in chicken broth, and stir continuously. Add the fish sauce and honey; simmer for 15 minutes.
3. **Add** the coconut milk, carrot, mushrooms, and green peas, and cook 8 to 10 minutes or until the mushrooms is soft.
4. **Stir** in the shrimp, and cook for about 5 minutes, or until no longer translucent. Drizzle soup with lime juice and season with salt.
5. **Sprinkle** chopped green onions and parsley over the top to serve.

# 33. Tropical Salad with Bacon

Servings: 3

Preparation time: 15 minutes

Cook time: 10 minutes

Ready in: 25 minutes

## Nutrition Facts

Serving Size 272 g

**Amount Per Serving**

**Calories** 433          Calories from Fat 230

| | % Daily Value* |
|---|---|
| **Total Fat** 25.6g | **39%** |
| Saturated Fat 6.2g | **31%** |
| *Trans* Fat 0.0g | |
| **Cholesterol** 14mg | **5%** |
| **Sodium** 626mg | **26%** |
| **Total Carbohydrates** 37.5g | **12%** |
| Dietary Fiber 4.2g | **17%** |
| Sugars 26.3g | |
| **Protein** 7.8g | |

| | | |
|---|---|---|
| Vitamin A 11% | • | Vitamin C 55% |
| Calcium 5% | • | Iron 13% |

**Nutrition Grade C+**

* Based on a 2000 calorie diet

## Ingredients

- 6 slices nitrite/nitrate free bacon
- 1/4 cup pure pineapple juice
- 1/4 cup olive oil
- 3 tablespoons rice wine vinegar
- 2 cloves garlic, crushed and chopped
- 1 thumb-size ginger, chopped
- 1/2 teaspoon sea salt
- 1/4 teaspoon freshly ground black pepper
- 1 (10 ounce) package chopped romaine lettuce
- 1 cup cubed fresh pineapple
- 1/2 cup raisins
- 1/2 cup chopped and toasted almonds
- 1/4 cup toasted coconut flakes

## Directions

1. **Place** bacon in a large skillet over medium-high heat. Cook 10 minutes, or until evenly browned. Drain, crumble, and set aside.
2. **Stir** together the pineapple juice, olive oil, rice wine vinegar, garlic, ginger, salt, and pepper.
3. **Combine** the cooked bacon, lettuce, pineapple, raisins, almonds, and coconut flakes in a large bowl.
4. **Pour** prepared dressing over salad, toss to coat and serve.

## 34. Coconut Crusted Deep Fried Shrimp

Servings: 5
Preparation time: 40 minutes
Cook time: 15 minutes
Ready in: 55 minutes

# Nutrition Facts

Serving Size 202 g

**Amount Per Serving**

| Calories 394 | Calories from Fat 228 |
|---|---|

| | % Daily Value* |
|---|---|
| **Total Fat** 25.3g | **39%** |
| Saturated Fat 20.7g | **104%** |
| **Cholesterol** 255mg | **85%** |
| **Sodium** 280mg | **12%** |
| **Total Carbohydrates** 8.1g | **3%** |
| Dietary Fiber 3.3g | **13%** |
| Sugars 2.6g | |
| **Protein** 26.6g | |

| Vitamin A 7% | • | Vitamin C 4% |
|---|---|---|
| Calcium 17% | • | Iron 30% |

**Nutrition Grade C+**
* Based on a 2000 calorie diet

### Ingredients

- 1 egg
- 1/3 cup coconut milk
- 1/3 cup coconut rum
- 3/4 cup gluten-free all-purpose flour
- 1 1/2 teaspoons gluten-free baking powder

- 2 cups flaked coconut
- 24 shrimps, peeled and deveined
- 3 cups melted coconut oil for deep frying

## Directions

1. **Line** a baking sheet with wax paper.
2. **Whisk** together the egg, coconut milk, coconut rum, 1/2 cup flour, and baking powder in a shallow dish.
3. **Place** the coconut and remaining flour in two separate bowls.
4. **Dredge** shrimp in flour, shaking off excess flour. Dip in egg mixture, and then roll shrimp in coconut.
5. **Place** coated shrimps on the prepared baking sheet. Refrigerate for 30 minutes.
6. **Heat** coconut oil in a deep-fryer.
7. **Fry** shrimps for 2 to 3 minutes or until golden brown; turning once.
8. **Drain** cooked shrimps on paper towels.

# 35. Chicken Satay with Peanut Sauce

Servings: 5

Preparation time: 30 minutes

Cook time: 30 minutes

Ready in: 1 hour

## Nutrition Facts

Serving Size 245 g

**Amount Per Serving**

**Calories** 419      Calories from Fat 289

|  | % Daily Value* |
|---|---|
| **Total Fat** 32.1g | **49%** |
| Saturated Fat 18.4g | **92%** |
| Trans Fat 0.0g | |
| **Cholesterol** 39mg | **13%** |
| **Sodium** 780mg | **33%** |
| **Total Carbohydrates** 23.4g | **8%** |
| Dietary Fiber 4.0g | **16%** |
| Sugars 6.7g | |
| **Protein** 23.0g | |

| Vitamin A 2% | • | Vitamin C 9% |
|---|---|---|
| Calcium 3% | • | Iron 13% |

**Nutrition Grade C+**

* Based on a 2000 calorie diet

## Ingredients

- 1 clove garlic, minced
- 1 tablespoon chopped ginger
- 1 1/2 tablespoons curry powder
- 1 1/2 teaspoons raw honey
- 1/2 teaspoon sea salt
- 1/2 teaspoon ground black pepper
- 1 1/2 cup coconut milk
- 3/4 pound skinless, boneless chicken breast halves - cut into 1 inch strips
- 1/2 cup creamy peanut butter
- 3/4 cup low-sodium chicken broth
- 1/4 cup stevia
- 2 tablespoons lemon juice
- 1 teaspoon gluten-free soy sauce

- 1/2 teaspoon crushed red pepper flakes
- 1/2 teaspoon sea salt
- 10 (6 inch) wooden skewers

## Directions

1. **Soak** the skewers in water for 30 minutes.
2. **Place** chicken strips in a large bowl.
3. **Combine** the garlic, ginger, 1/2 tablespoon curry powder, honey, salt, pepper, and 1/2 cup coconut milk.
4. **Pour** mixture over the chicken and toss to coat. Cover, and marinate in the refrigerator for at least 30 minutes.
5. **Combine** the remaining coconut milk and curry powder, peanut butter, chicken broth, and stevia in a saucepan over medium-high heat.
6. **Simmer** for 5 minutes, stirring constantly until smooth and thickened. Remove pan from heat and stir in lemon juice, soy sauce, red pepper flakes, and salt.
7. **Preheat** a grill for medium-high heat.
8. **Thread** marinated chicken onto skewers. Grill chicken for 5 minutes per side, or until cooked through.
9. **Serve** with warm peanut sauce.

## 36. Zesty Coconut Burgers

Servings: 8

Preparation time: 20 minutes

Cook time: 15 minutes

Ready in: 35 minutes

## Nutrition Facts

Serving Size 189 g

**Amount Per Serving**

**Calories** 443      Calories from Fat 256

| | % Daily Value* |
|---|---|
| **Total Fat** 28.4g | **44%** |
| Saturated Fat 13.3g | **67%** |
| *Trans* Fat 0.0g | |
| **Cholesterol** 79mg | **26%** |
| **Sodium** 912mg | **38%** |
| **Total Carbohydrates** 25.6g | **9%** |
| Dietary Fiber 2.5g | **10%** |
| Sugars 3.7g | |
| **Protein** 21.6g | |

| | | |
|---|---|---|
| Vitamin A 6% | • | Vitamin C 9% |
| Calcium 1% | • | Iron 64% |

**Nutrition Grade C**

* Based on a 2000 calorie diet

### Ingredients

- 1 pound ground beef
- 1 1/2 cup unsweetened shredded dried coconut
- 1 egg
- 1/3 cup chopped fresh parsley
- 2 tablespoons gluten-free Worcestershire sauce
- 2 tablespoons lime juice
- 1 tablespoon lime zest
- 1 1/2 tablespoons coconut cream
- 1 teaspoon coconut aminos
- 2 teaspoons sea salt
- 1 cup low-fat mayonnaise
- 1 tablespoon olive oil, plus extra amount for greasing
- 1/4 cup gluten-free oatmeal
- 4 gluten-free hamburger buns, split

120

**Directions**

1. **Combine** the beef, 1/2 cup coconut, egg, 1/4 cup parsley, Worcestershire sauce, lime juice, lime zest, 1 tablespoon coconut cream, coconut aminos, and 1 1/2 teaspoons salt in a bowl.
2. **Shape** mixture into 4 patties, and set aside.
3. **Whisk** together the mayonnaise with the remaining coconut cream and parsley.
4. **Heat** the olive oil in a skillet over medium heat. Stir in the oatmeal, and remaining coconut and salt, cook until golden brown. Drain on a paper towels and set aside.
5. **Preheat** an outdoor grill for medium-high heat, and lightly oil grate with olive oil.
6. **Grill** the patties for about 4 minutes per side.
7. **Place** the cooked patties on the bottom buns then spread with parsley mayonnaise over the top. Sprinkle with the toasted coconut, and serve.

## 37. Pan Seared Garam Masala Tilapia with Coconut-Curry Sauce

Servings: 8

Preparation time: 15 minutes

Cook time: 20 minutes

Ready in: 35 minutes

**Nutrition Facts**

Serving Size 260 g

Amount Per Serving

Calories 338 — Calories from Fat 188

% Daily Value*

| | |
|---|---|
| Total Fat 20.9g | 32% |
| Saturated Fat 10.1g | 50% |
| Trans Fat 0.0g | |
| Cholesterol 83mg | 28% |
| Sodium 302mg | 13% |
| Total Carbohydrates 2.9g | 1% |
| Dietary Fiber 0.5g | 2% |
| Sugars 0.9g | |
| Protein 34.2g | |

Vitamin A 0%  •  Vitamin C 5%

Calcium 4%  •  Iron 14%

**Nutrition Grade D-**

* Based on a 2000 calorie diet

### Ingredients

- 1/2 cup rice wine vinegar
- 1/4 cup pure apple juice
- 1 cup lite coconut milk
- 2 tablespoons curry powder
- 1 cup cold, unsalted butter, cut into cubes
- 1/2 teaspoon sea salt
- 1/4 cup olive oil, or to taste
- 8 (6 ounce) tilapia fillets
- 2 tablespoons garam masala

## Directions

1. **Pour** rice wine vinegar, apple juice, coconut milk, and curry powder into a saucepan over medium-high heat. Bring to a boil, and then reduce heat to medium-low.

2. **Simmer** for about 10 minutes, or until the liquid has reduced to 1/2 cup.

3. **Reduce** heat to low, and whisk in the butter, a few cubes at a time, until incorporated. Season with salt to taste then set aside.

4. **Heat** the olive oil in a skillet over medium-high heat. Season both sides of the tilapia with garam masala and salt.

5. **Sear** the fish in the hot oil for 3 minutes on each side. Drain on paper towels.

6. **Serve** with the coconut-curry sauce.

## 38. Coconut Chicken with Gravy

Servings: 5

Preparation time: 40 minutes

Cook time: 40 minutes

Ready in: 1 hour and 20 minutes

**Nutrition Facts**

Serving Size 309 g

**Amount Per Serving**

Calories 451 — Calories from Fat 191

% Daily Value*

| | |
|---|---|
| Total Fat 21.2g | 33% |
| Saturated Fat 15.6g | 78% |
| Trans Fat 0.0g | |
| Cholesterol 112mg | 37% |
| Sodium 547mg | 23% |
| Total Carbohydrates 30.4g | 10% |
| Dietary Fiber 3.9g | 16% |
| Sugars 7.6g | |
| Protein 34.0g | |

| | |
|---|---|
| Vitamin A 1% | Vitamin C 5% |
| Calcium 2% | Iron 7% |

**Nutrition Grade D+**

* Based on a 2000 calorie diet

### Ingredients

- 1 cup coconut milk, divided
- 1 clove garlic, minced
- 1 tablespoon coconut aminos
- 1 tablespoon lemon juice
- 1 1/2 pounds skinless, boneless chicken breast halves, cut into strips
- 1/2 cup gluten-free all-purpose flour
- 1 egg, beaten
- 1 cup sweetened desiccated coconut
- 1 cup gluten-free panko bread crumbs
- 1/2 teaspoon sea salt
- 1/2 teaspoon ground black pepper
- 1 cup low-sodium chicken broth
- 1 tablespoon low-fat butter

124

- 1 tablespoon gluten-free cornstarch
- olive oil for greasing

## Directions

1. **Stir** together the coconut milk, garlic, coconut aminos, and lemon juice in a large mixing bowl.
2. **Add** the chicken strips and toss to coat with marinade. Refrigerate for at least 30 minutes
3. **Preheat** oven to 400 degrees F (200 degrees C). Line a baking sheet with aluminum foil and grease with olive oil.
4. **Place** the flour into a shallow bowl and the egg into another bowl.
5. **Mix** together the desiccated coconut, panko crumbs, salt, and black pepper in a third bowl. **Dredge** the marinated chicken strips into the flour to evenly coat. Dip into egg, and finally into the coconut crumb mixture. Place the coated strips onto the prepared baking sheet.
6. **Bake** the chicken strips for 30 minutes, or until golden brown.
7. **Heat** the chicken broth and butter in a saucepan over medium heat. Add the cornstarch and bring to a boil; stirring frequently. Pour mixture into a small bowl and serve with coconut chicken strips.

# 39. Coconut Curry Tofu and Mushrooms with Coconut Rice

Servings: 2

Preparation time: 10 minutes

Cook time: 30 minutes

Ready in: 40 minutes

## Nutrition Facts

Serving Size 325 g

**Amount Per Serving**

| | |
|---|---|
| **Calories** 499 | Calories from Fat 239 |

| | % Daily Value* |
|---|---|
| **Total Fat** 26.6g | **41%** |
| Saturated Fat 20.3g | **101%** |
| **Cholesterol** 0mg | **0%** |
| **Sodium** 503mg | **21%** |
| **Total Carbohydrates** 56.5g | **19%** |
| Dietary Fiber 6.1g | **25%** |
| Sugars 7.9g | |
| **Protein** 13.3g | |

| | | |
|---|---|---|
| Vitamin A 7% | • | Vitamin C 32% |
| Calcium 14% | • | Iron 28% |

**Nutrition Grade B-**

* Based on a 2000 calorie diet

## Ingredients

- 1/2 cup water
- 3/4 cup coconut milk
- 1/2 cup uncooked basmati rice
- 1/2 teaspoon low-fat butter
- 1 clove garlic, minced
- 2 tablespoons minced fresh ginger
- 3 ounces firm tofu, cubed
- 1 cup sliced fresh mushrooms
- 1/2 cup green peas
- 1/4 teaspoon curry powder
- 1/2 teaspoon raw honey
- 1 pinch chili powder
- 1/2 teaspoon sea salt

- 1 tablespoon chopped cashews

## Directions

1. **Pour** water, 1/2 cup coconut milk, and rice into a small saucepan over medium-high heat.
2. **Bring** to a boil, and then reduce heat to medium-low. Simmer covered for 20 minutes, or until rice is tender.
3. **Melt** the butter in a skillet over medium-high heat. Add the garlic and ginger and sauté until lightly browned.
4. **Stir** in the tofu and cook for 5 minutes, or until golden-brown on all sides. Add the mushrooms, green peas, curry powder, honey, chili powder, salt, and remaining coconut milk.
5. **Simmer** until the vegetables are tender.
6. **Sprinkle** with chopped cashews over the top and then serve over rice.

## 40. Spicy Lime Pork

Servings: 4

Preparation time: 15 minutes

Cook time: 20 minutes

Ready in: 35 minutes

```
Nutrition Facts
Serving Size 434 g

Amount Per Serving
Calories 414          Calories from Fat 167
                              % Daily Value*
Total Fat 18.6g                          29%
   Saturated Fat 7.5g                    38%
   Trans Fat 0.1g
Cholesterol 124mg                        41%
Sodium 366mg                             15%
Total Carbohydrates 14.5g                 5%
   Dietary Fiber 6.0g                    24%
   Sugars 4.5g
Protein 47.7g

Vitamin A 13%          •       Vitamin C 68%
Calcium 4%             •           Iron 18%
Nutrition Grade A-
* Based on a 2000 calorie diet
```

### Ingredients

- 1 1/2 pound pork tenderloin, cut into 1/2" strips
- 1/2 teaspoon sea salt
- 1/4 teaspoon freshly ground black pepper
- 1 1/2 tablespoon coconut oil
- 2 red onion, chopped
- 1 cup cauliflower florets
- 2 small jalapeno, chopped
- 1 cup low-sodium chicken broth
- 1/2 cup diced tomatoes
- 1/3 cup lime juice
- 1/3 cup parsley, chopped
- 1 avocado, sliced
- 16 butter lettuce leaves

### Directions

1.  **Place** pork in a large bowl then season with salt and pepper.
2.  **Heat** coconut oil in a large skillet over medium-high heat. Add pork and sauté until lightly browned, about 4 minutes. Drain then transfer cooked pork into a bowl and set aside.
3.  **Sauté** onion, cauliflower, and jalapeno in the hot pan until tender, about 8 minutes.
4.  **Pour** the chicken broth and add the tomatoes. Reduce heat to low and simmer for 2 minutes.
5.  **Add** pork and juices to pan. Stir in lime juice and simmer until pork is fully cooked.
6.  **Spoon** mixture onto lettuce leaves. Top with fresh parsley and avocado then roll up.

## 41. Honey Mustard Coconut Fish

Servings: 3

Preparation time: 10 minutes

Cook time: 20 minutes

Ready in: 30 minutes

# Nutrition Facts

Serving Size 216 g

**Amount Per Serving**

**Calories** 507 | Calories from Fat 250

% Daily Value*

**Total Fat** 27.7g | **43%**

Saturated Fat 12.4g | **62%**

*Trans* Fat 0.0g

**Cholesterol** 76mg | **25%**

**Sodium** 838mg | **35%**

**Total Carbohydrates** 20.9g | **7%**

Dietary Fiber 3.7g | **15%**

Sugars 7.4g

**Protein** 44.5g

Vitamin A 7% • Vitamin C 5%

Calcium 10% • Iron 23%

**Nutrition Grade B-**

* Based on a 2000 calorie diet

## Ingredients

- 1/4 cup pure mayonnaise
- 3 tablespoons mustard
- 1 tablespoon honey
- 1/2 cup gluten-free panko bread crumbs
- 1/4 cup coarsely chopped almonds
- 1/4 cup shredded coconut
- 1 teaspoon stevia
- 1 teaspoon sea salt
- 1/2 teaspoon crushed red pepper flakes
- 1/4 teaspoon ground black pepper
- 1 pound Swordfish fillets
- coconut oil for greasing

## Directions

1. **Preheat** oven to 375 degrees F (190 degrees C). Lightly grease a 9x13 inch baking dish with coconut oil.

2. **Blend** mayonnaise, mustard, and honey in a small bowl.

3. **Combine** bread crumbs, chopped almonds, shredded coconut, stevia, salt, red pepper flakes, and black pepper in a medium bowl.

4. **Dip** fish in the mayonnaise mixture, then in the bread crumb mixture. Arrange coated fish fillets in the prepared baking dish.

5. **Bake** 20 minutes, or until fish flakes easily with a fork.

## 42. Beef 'n Spinach Curry

Servings: 5

Preparation time: 10 minutes

Cook time: 45 minutes

Ready in: 55 minutes

# Nutrition Facts

Serving Size 314 g

**Amount Per Serving**

**Calories** 431       Calories from Fat 211

| | % Daily Value* |
|---|---|
| **Total Fat** 23.4g | **36%** |
| Saturated Fat 13.1g | **66%** |
| Trans Fat 0.0g | |
| **Cholesterol** 125mg | **42%** |
| **Sodium** 699mg | **29%** |
| **Total Carbohydrates** 12.8g | **4%** |
| Dietary Fiber 4.9g | **20%** |
| Sugars 4.3g | |
| **Protein** 43.3g | |

| | | |
|---|---|---|
| Vitamin A 185% | • | Vitamin C 48% |
| Calcium 12% | • | Iron 35% |

**Nutrition Grade A-**

* Based on a 2000 calorie diet

## Ingredients

- 2 tablespoons low-fat butter
- 2 cloves garlic, crushed
- 1 large onion, finely sliced
- 2 jalapeno peppers, thinly sliced

- 2 whole cloves, bruised
- 2 teaspoons ground cumin
- 1 teaspoon ground cilantro
- 1 teaspoon turmeric
- 1/2 teaspoon chili powder
- 1/2 teaspoon ground nutmeg
- 1 1/2 pounds beef tenderloin, cubed
- 1 teaspoon sea salt
- 2/3 cup coconut milk
- 1 (10 ounce) bag spinach
- 1 cup diced carrots
- 1/2 cup chopped tomatoes
- 1 teaspoon lime juice

**Directions**
1. **Heat** the butter in a large saucepan over medium heat.
2. **Add** the garlic and onion, sauté for about 5 minutes, or until onion has turned translucent. Stir in the jalapeno peppers, and cook for 3 minutes more.
3. **Season** with cloves, cumin, cilantro, turmeric, chili powder, and nutmeg; cook for additional 3 minutes.
4. **Add** the beef and salt, stir and cook for 3 minutes. Add the coconut milk, spinach, carrots, and chopped tomatoes.
5. **Cover**, and simmer for 20 minutes, stirring occasionally.
6. **Drizzle** soup with lime juice. Cook for 10 more minutes, or until the sauce has thickened; stirring frequently.

# DINNER

## 43. Thai Butternut Squash Soup

Servings: 4

Preparation time: 10 minutes

Cook time: 15 minutes

Ready in: 25 minutes

**Nutrition Facts**

Serving Size 504 g

| Amount Per Serving | |
|---|---|
| **Calories** 375 | Calories from Fat 238 |
| | **% Daily Value*** |
| **Total Fat** 26.5g | **41%** |
| Saturated Fat 20.4g | **102%** |
| **Cholesterol** 0mg | **0%** |
| **Sodium** 73mg | **3%** |
| **Total Carbohydrates** 34.1g | **11%** |
| Dietary Fiber 7.4g | **30%** |
| Sugars 11.2g | |
| **Protein** 6.2g | |

| | | | |
|---|---|---|---|
| Vitamin A 308% | • | Vitamin C 105% | |
| Calcium 9% | • | Iron 16% | |

**Nutrition Grade B**

* Based on a 2000 calorie diet

## Ingredients

- 1 tablespoon olive oil
- 1 tablespoon low-fat butter
- 1 clove garlic, chopped
- 4 medium red onions, chopped
- 1/2 red bell pepper, chopped
- 1/4 teaspoon crushed red pepper flakes
- 1 tablespoon chopped lemon grass
- 1 thumb-size fresh ginger, chopped
- 2 1/4 cups low-sodium chicken broth
- 4 cups peeled and diced butternut squash
- 1 1/2 cups unsweetened coconut milk
- 2 teaspoons fresh lime juice

- fresh basil leaves for garnish

## Directions
1. **Heat** the olive oil and butter in a medium saucepan over low heat.
2. **Stir** in garlic, onions, bell pepper, red pepper flakes, lemongrass, and ginger, sauté until garlic has turned golden brown.
3. **Pour** in chicken broth, coconut milk, and squash, and then bring to a boil. Cook until squash softens, about 10 to 15 minutes.
4. **Pour** the soup in a blender and blend (in batches) until smooth but slightly chunky.
5. **Drizzle** soup with few drops of lime juice and garnish with basil leaves. Serve warm.

## 44. Spicy Mongolian Beef

Servings: 3

Preparation time: 40 minutes

Cook time: 8 minutes

Ready in: 48 minutes

## Nutrition Facts

Serving Size 197 g

**Amount Per Serving**

| | |
|---|---|
| **Calories** 389 | Calories from Fat 172 |

| | % Daily Value* |
|---|---|
| **Total Fat** 19.1g | **29%** |
| Saturated Fat 8.3g | **42%** |
| *Trans* Fat 0.0g | |
| **Cholesterol** 135mg | **45%** |
| **Sodium** 253mg | **11%** |
| **Total Carbohydrates** 6.9g | **2%** |
| Dietary Fiber 1.1g | **4%** |
| Sugars 2.0g | |
| **Protein** 46.8g | |

| | | |
|---|---|---|
| Vitamin A 18% | • | Vitamin C 9% |
| Calcium 2% | • | Iron 161% |

**Nutrition Grade B**

* Based on a 2000 calorie diet

## Ingredients

- 1/4 cup gluten-free soy sauce
- 1 tablespoon hoisin sauce
- 1 tablespoon sesame oil
- 2 teaspoons stevia
- 1 tablespoon minced garlic
- 1 tablespoon dried cayenne pepper
- 1 pound beef flank steak, thinly sliced
- 1 tablespoon melted coconut oil
- 2 large green onions, thinly sliced

## Directions

1. **Whisk** together soy sauce, hoisin sauce, sesame oil, stevia, garlic, and cayenne pepper in a bowl.

2. **Pour** mixture over beef and toss to coat. Cover, and marinate in the refrigerator for at least 30 minutes, or overnight for best flavor.

3. **Heat** coconut oil in a large skillet over high heat. Stir in the green onions and the marinated beef.

4. **Cook** beef for 5 minutes, or until no longer pink and evenly browned; stirring frequently.

## 45. Savory Coconut Tofu Keema

Servings: 7
Preparation time: 10 minutes
Cook time: 40 minutes
Ready in: 50 minutes

## Nutrition Facts

Serving Size 446 g

**Amount Per Serving**

**Calories** 383      Calories from Fat 256

|  | % Daily Value* |
| --- | --- |
| **Total Fat** 28.5g | **44%** |
| Saturated Fat 16.1g | **81%** |
| Trans Fat 0.0g | |
| **Cholesterol** 0mg | **0%** |
| **Sodium** 1429mg | **60%** |
| **Total Carbohydrates** 27.4g | **9%** |
| Dietary Fiber 8.5g | **34%** |
| Sugars 15.5g | |
| **Protein** 11.7g | |

| | | |
| --- | --- | --- |
| Vitamin A 111% | • | Vitamin C 47% |
| Calcium 17% | • | Iron 29% |

**Nutrition Grade A-**
* Based on a 2000 calorie diet

### Ingredients

- 1/4 cup olive oil
- 4 cloves garlic, pressed
- 1 medium onions, minced
- 1 (14 ounce) package extra firm tofu, diced
- 2 cups coconut milk
- 1 1/2 tablespoons curry paste

136

- 1 1/2 teaspoons ground ginger
- 1 teaspoon sea salt
- 1/2 tablespoon crushed red pepper flakes
- 6 cups organic tomato sauce
- 1 1/2 cups frozen peas, thawed
- 1 cup chopped tomatoes
- 1 1/2 cups chopped carrots

## Directions

1. **Heat** olive oil in a large saucepan over medium heat. Add garlic, onion, and tofu, cook for 5 to 10 minutes; stirring occasionally.
2. **Stir** in coconut milk, curry paste, ginger, salt, and red pepper flakes; bring mixture to a simmer.
3. **Pour** in tomato sauce, peas, tomatoes, and carrots.
4. **Cover** pan and simmer for 30 minutes.

# 46. Zucchini and Meatballs

Servings: 3

Preparation time: 15 minutes

Cook time: 30 minutes

Ready in: 45 minutes

## Nutrition Facts

Serving Size 585 g

**Amount Per Serving**

**Calories** 421      Calories from Fat 136

| | % Daily Value* |
|---|---|
| **Total Fat** 15.1g | **23%** |
|   Saturated Fat 7.7g | **38%** |
| **Cholesterol** 135mg | **45%** |
| **Sodium** 1601mg | **67%** |
| **Total Carbohydrates** 21.8g | **7%** |
|   Dietary Fiber 7.0g | **28%** |
|   Sugars 12.6g | |
| **Protein** 51.9g | |

| | | |
|---|---|---|
| Vitamin A 29% | • | Vitamin C 104% |
| Calcium 10% | • | Iron 191% |

**Nutrition Grade A**

* Based on a 2000 calorie diet

## Ingredients

- 1 pound lean ground beef
- 2 cloves garlic, minced
- 2 tablespoons dried oregano
- 1/4 cup chopped parsley
- 1 teaspoon sea salt
- 1/4 teaspoon ground black pepper
- 1 tablespoon coconut oil
- 1/2 yellow onion, diced
- 2 medium zucchini, diced
- 1 cup sliced fresh mushrooms
- 2 medium tomatoes, diced
- 2 cups organic tomato sauce

## Directions

1. **Combine** the ground beef, garlic, oregano, parsley, 1/2 teaspoon salt, and pepper in a bowl.
2. **Shape** the mixture into 1 inch balls.
3. **Heat** coconut oil in a large skillet over medium-high heat. Add the onions and sauté until slightly translucent.
4. **Add** the meatballs and cook for about 5 minutes, or until golden browned.
5. **Stir** in the zucchini, mushrooms, and tomatoes and continue to cook until tender. Pour in the tomato sauce and season with remaining salt; simmer until heated through.

## 47. Honey Coconut Crusted Salmon

Servings: 4

Preparation time: 40 minutes

Cook time: 25 minutes

Ready in: 1 hour and 5 minutes

## Nutrition Facts

Serving Size 264 g

**Amount Per Serving**

| | |
|---|---|
| **Calories** 599 | Calories from Fat 335 |

**% Daily Value\***

| | |
|---|---|
| **Total Fat** 37.2g | **57%** |
| Saturated Fat 23.4g | **117%** |
| _Trans_ Fat 0.0g | |
| **Cholesterol** 24mg | **8%** |
| **Sodium** 476mg | **20%** |
| **Total Carbohydrates** 52.1g | **17%** |
| Dietary Fiber 2.3g | **9%** |
| Sugars 37.0g | |
| **Protein** 31.7g | |

| | | |
|---|---|---|
| Vitamin A 4% | • | Vitamin C 9% |
| Calcium 1% | • | Iron 16% |

**Nutrition Grade D+**

\* Based on a 2000 calorie diet

## Ingredients

- 3/4 cup low-fat butter
- 1/2 cup coconut milk

139

- 1/2 cup raw honey
- 1/4 cup stevia
- 3/4 cup coconut flakes
- 1/4 cup chopped onions
- 1/2 teaspoon sea salt
- 1/4 teaspoon ground black pepper
- 4 (4 ounce) fillets salmon

### Directions

1. **Melt** the butter in a saucepan over medium heat.
2. **Pour** in the coconut milk, honey, stevia, coconut flakes, onions, salt, and pepper; bring mixture to a boil. Remove pan from heat and cool slightly then transfer mixture to a large bowl.
3. **Add** the salmon, and turn to coat evenly. Cover, and marinate in the refrigerator for at least 30 minutes.
4. **Preheat** oven to 375 degrees F (190 degrees C).
5. **Spread** half of the marinade mixture in the bottom of a baking dish. Arrange the salmon in a single layer on top of the marinade, and pour remaining half of the marinade over the top.
6. **Bake** for 25 minutes or until the salmon flakes easily with a fork.

## 48. Apple Raspberry Chicken and Coconut Rice

Servings: 6

Preparation time: 15 minutes

Cook time: 25 minutes

Ready in: 40 minutes

**Nutrition Facts**

Serving Size 341 g

**Amount Per Serving**

| | |
|---|---|
| **Calories** 541 | Calories from Fat 218 |

**% Daily Value\***

| | |
|---|---|
| **Total Fat** 24.2g | **37%** |
| Saturated Fat 19.3g | **97%** |
| *Trans* Fat 0.0g | |
| **Cholesterol** 66mg | **22%** |
| **Sodium** 199mg | **8%** |
| **Total Carbohydrates** 53.1g | **18%** |
| Dietary Fiber 2.9g | **11%** |
| Sugars 17.2g | |
| **Protein** 28.0g | |

| | | |
|---|---|---|
| Vitamin A 0% | • | Vitamin C 13% |
| Calcium 3% | • | Iron 10% |

**Nutrition Grade C-**

\* Based on a 2000 calorie diet

### Ingredients

- 2 cups water
- 1 3/4 cup reduced-fat coconut milk
- 1 clove garlic, minced
- 2 teaspoons minced fresh ginger root
- 1 cup basmati rice
- 1/3 cup gluten-free all-purpose flour
- 1 tablespoon lemon zest
- 4 (6 ounce) skinless, boneless chicken breast half - cut into bite-size pieces
- 2 tablespoons coconut oil, melted
- 2 teaspoons dried thyme
- 1/4 cup apple juice
- 1 tablespoon apple cider vinegar
- 1/2 cup pure raspberry jam

141

**Directions**

1. **Place** the water, coconut milk, garlic, ginger, and rice in a large pot over medium high heat.
2. **Cover**, and simmer for about 15 minutes until all liquid is absorbed, stirring occasionally.
3. **Mix** together the flour, lemon zest in a shallow dish. Dredge chicken in the flour mixture.
4. **Heat** coconut oil in a large skillet over medium heat. Add the coated chicken strips and thyme, cook until golden brown, turning occasionally. Transfer cooked chicken pieces to a plate, and set aside.
5. **Pour** apple juice, apple cider vinegar, and raspberry jam into the skillet, and simmer, stirring occasionally, until liquid is reduced by half. Return chicken to skillet, and cook until all liquid is absorbed.
6. **Serve** chicken with coconut rice.

## 49. Caribbean Coconut Chicken

Servings: 4

Preparation time: 15 minutes

Cook time: 55 minutes

Ready in: 1 hour and 10 minutes

## Nutrition Facts

Serving Size 311 g

**Amount Per Serving**

| | |
|---|---|
| **Calories** 380 | Calories from Fat 177 |

| | % Daily Value* |
|---|---|
| **Total Fat** 19.7g | **30%** |
| Saturated Fat 13.7g | **68%** |
| **Cholesterol** 99mg | **33%** |
| **Sodium** 520mg | **22%** |
| **Total Carbohydrates** 10.8g | **4%** |
| Dietary Fiber 3.3g | **13%** |
| Sugars 5.1g | |
| **Protein** 37.4g | |

| | | |
|---|---|---|
| Vitamin A 39% | • | Vitamin C 137% |
| Calcium 2% | • | Iron 9% |

**Nutrition Grade C**

* Based on a 2000 calorie diet

## Ingredients

- 4 (6-ounce) skinless, boneless chicken breasts
- 1 teaspoon olive oil
- 1/4 cup chopped onions
- 2 tablespoons grated fresh ginger
- 2 red bell peppers, chopped
- 1 jalapeno pepper
- 1 tablespoon chopped roasted garlic
- 1 teaspoon dried cilantro
- 1 cup coconut milk
- 1 tablespoon fresh lime juice
- 1/2 teaspoon sea salt
- 1/4 teaspoon ground black pepper
- 1/4 teaspoon crushed red pepper flakes

### Directions

1.  **Preheat** oven to 425 degrees F (220 degrees C).
2.  **Heat** olive oil in a large skillet over medium heat. Add the chicken and fry until just begins to brown.
3.  **Stir** in the onions, ginger, bell peppers, and jalapeno pepper; sauté until the onions are translucent.
4.  **Add** the garlic and cilantro then pour in coconut milk and lime juice; simmer for 5 to 8 minutes. Remove skillet from the heat, then season the mixture with salt, black pepper, and red pepper flakes. Transfer the mixture to a 9x13 inch baking dish.
5.  **Bake** 45 minutes, or until the chicken is tender.

## 50. Indian Dahl with Spinach

Servings: 4

Preparation time: 15 minutes

Cook time: 40 minutes

Ready in: 55 minutes

## Nutrition Facts

Serving Size 514 g

**Amount Per Serving**

**Calories** 565     Calories from Fat 182

|  | % Daily Value* |
| --- | --- |
| **Total Fat** 20.2g | **31%** |
| Saturated Fat 14.7g | **73%** |
| *Trans* Fat 0.0g | |
| **Cholesterol** 0mg | **0%** |
| **Sodium** 382mg | **16%** |
| **Total Carbohydrates** 70.5g | **23%** |
| Dietary Fiber 31.9g | **128%** |
| Sugars 7.5g | |
| **Protein** 29.1g | |

| Vitamin A 218% | • | Vitamin C 67% |
| --- | --- | --- |
| Calcium 20% | • | Iron 63% |

**Nutrition Grade A**

* Based on a 2000 calorie diet

### Ingredients

*   1 1/2 cups red lentils
*   1/2 cup chickpeas

- 3 1/2 cups water
- 1/2 teaspoon sea salt
- 1/2 teaspoon ground turmeric
- 3/4 teaspoon hot pepper sauce
- 1/4 teaspoon dried oregano
- 1 pound spinach, rinsed and chopped
- 2 tablespoons low-fat butter
- 1 onion, chopped
- 3/4 teaspoon curry powder
- 1 teaspoon chili powder
- 1 teaspoon mustard powder
- 1/2 cup coconut milk
- 1 teaspoon garam masala
- 1/2 cup unsweetened shredded coconut

## Directions

1. **Rinse** the lentils and chickpeas then soak in water for 20 minutes.
2. **Boil** the 3 1/2 cups of water in a large saucepan over medium heat. Stir in lentils, chickpeas, salt, turmeric, hot pepper sauce, and oregano.
3. **Cover** pan and return mixture to a boil. Turn heat to Low and simmer for 15 minutes. Add the spinach and cook for 5 minutes.
4. **Melt** butter in a small saucepan over medium heat. Add the onions and curry powder and let caramelize for 15 minutes on Low heat.
5. **Stir** in the chili powder and mustard powder. Combine onion mixture with lentil mixture.
6. **Pour** in coconut milk then add the garam masala and coconut; cook until heated through.

## 51. Bengali Shrimp Curry

Servings: 8

Preparation time: 15 minutes

Cook time: 23 minutes

Ready in: 38 minutes

**Nutrition Facts**

Serving Size 216 g

**Amount Per Serving**

**Calories** 359     Calories from Fat 280

|  | % Daily Value* |
|---|---|
| **Total Fat** 31.1g | **48%** |
| Saturated Fat 24.1g | **121%** |
| *Trans* Fat 0.0g | |
| **Cholesterol** 81mg | **27%** |
| **Sodium** 224mg | **9%** |
| **Total Carbohydrates** 11.2g | **4%** |
| Dietary Fiber 3.8g | **15%** |
| Sugars 5.7g | |
| **Protein** 13.5g | |

Vitamin A 7%    •    Vitamin C 9%

Calcium 2%    •    Iron 19%

**Nutrition Grade C+**

* Based on a 2000 calorie diet

## Ingredients

- 1 pound large shrimp, peeled and deveined
- 1/2 teaspoon sea salt
- 1 teaspoon turmeric powder
- 2 1/2 tablespoons mustard oil
- 1 large bay leaf
- 1 teaspoon ginger garlic paste
- 1 medium onion, finely chopped
- 1/2 teaspoon ground red chili pepper
- 1 cup water
- 1 3/4 cup coconut milk
- 1 teaspoon raw honey
- 1 teaspoon garam masala
- 1 cup shredded coconut
- 1/4 cup diced green chilies

146

- 1 1/2 cup coconut cream
- 3 tablespoons chopped fresh cilantro

**Directions**

1. **Season** shrimp with the salt and 1/2 teaspoon of turmeric powder. Set aside.
2. **Heat** 1 1/2 tablespoons of mustard oil in a skillet over medium heat. Add shrimp and sauté until pink and cooked through, about 5 minutes. Remove cooked shrimp from skillet and set aside.
3. **Heat** the remaining mustard oil in the same skillet. Add the bay leaf and ginger garlic paste. Stir in the onions and cook until translucent.
4. **Add** the red chili pepper and remaining turmeric powder. Cover with a cup of water and cook for 1 more minute.
5. **Stir** in the coconut milk, honey, and garam masala, cover and bring to a boil. Add the shrimp, cover and cook for about 10 minutes. Add the shredded coconut and green chili; bring to a boil.
6. **Remove** skillet from heat and stir in the coconut cream. Garnish with chopped cilantro to serve.

## 52. Thai-Style Pork Tenderloin with Peanut Sauce

Servings: 4

Preparation time: 12 minutes

Cook time: 20 minutes

Ready in: 32 minutes

**Nutrition Facts**

Serving Size 298 g

**Amount Per Serving**

| | |
|---|---|
| **Calories** 549 | Calories from Fat 257 |

| | % Daily Value* |
|---|---|
| **Total Fat** 28.5g | **44%** |
| Saturated Fat 11.0g | **55%** |
| *Trans* Fat 0.1g | |
| **Cholesterol** 146mg | **49%** |
| **Sodium** 518mg | **22%** |
| **Total Carbohydrates** 14.9g | **5%** |
| Dietary Fiber 2.3g | **9%** |
| Sugars 6.9g | |
| **Protein** 57.9g | |

| | | |
|---|---|---|
| Vitamin A 7% | • | Vitamin C 17% |
| Calcium 3% | • | Iron 23% |

**Nutrition Grade B**

* Based on a 2000 calorie diet

### Ingredients

- 1/4 cup gluten-free all-purpose flour
- 1 teaspoon ground cumin
- 1/4 teaspoon ground red pepper
- 1/2 teaspoon sea salt
- 2 tablespoons sesame oil
- 4 (7-ounce) pork tenderloin
- 1/3 cup low-sodium chicken broth
- 1/2 cup light coconut milk
- 2 tablespoons natural peanut butter
- 1 tablespoon raw honey
- 1 tablespoon minced garlic
- 1 teaspoon ground ginger
- 1/4 teaspoon sea salt

148

- 1/4 cup coarsely chopped dry roasted cashews
- 1/4 cup chopped green onion
- 1/4 cup sliced red bell pepper
- 1/4 cup chopped fresh cilantro

## Directions

1. **Mix** together the flour, cumin, ground red pepper and 1/2 teaspoon of salt in a plate or shallow dish. Dredge pork in the flour mixture to evenly coat, and shake off any excess.
2. **Heat** the sesame oil in a large skillet over medium-high heat. Add the coated pork and fry for 4 minutes per side, until cooked through. Transfer pork to a serving platter, and keep warm.
3. **Stir** together the chicken broth, coconut milk, peanut butter, honey, garlic, ginger, and 1/4 teaspoon of salt. Pour the sauce into the skillet and cook for 2 minutes, or until thickened; stirring constantly.
4. **Pour** peanut sauce over the pork, and garnish with cashews, green onion, bell pepper, and cilantro.

# 53. Hot Curried Tofu and Mangoes

Servings: 5

Preparation time: 15 minutes

Cook time: 15 minutes

Ready in: 30 minutes

## Nutrition Facts

Serving Size 308 g

**Amount Per Serving**

**Calories** 369 — Calories from Fat 246

% Daily Value*

**Total Fat** 27.3g — **42%**

Saturated Fat 19.0g — **95%**

**Cholesterol** 0mg — **0%**

**Sodium** 216mg — **9%**

**Total Carbohydrates** 28.4g — **9%**

Dietary Fiber 7.0g — **28%**

Sugars 17.8g

**Protein** 10.2g

Vitamin A 31% • Vitamin C 102%

Calcium 21% • Iron 25%

**Nutrition Grade B+**

* Based on a 2000 calorie diet

## Ingredients

- 1 tablespoon sesame oil
- 5 cloves garlic, minced
- 1 tablespoon minced ginger
- 1 medium red onion, minced
- 1 red bell pepper, seeded and diced
- 2 firm mangoes, peeled, seeded and sliced
- 1/4 cup yellow curry powder
- 1/2 teaspoon cayenne pepper
- 2 tablespoons chopped cilantro
- 1 3/4 cup light coconut milk
- 1 (14 ounce) package extra firm tofu, cubed
- 1/2 teaspoon sea salt
- 1/4 teaspoon ground black pepper
- 1 tablespoon fresh lime juice

- fresh cilantro leaves for garnish (optional)

**Directions**

1. **Heat** the sesame oil in a large pan over medium-high heat.
2. **Sauté** the garlic and ginger in hot oil until light browned, about 1 minute. Stir in the onion and bell pepper and cook until onion is translucent.
3. **Add** the mango and cook for another minute to soften slightly. Sprinkle with the curry powder, cayenne pepper, and cilantro; stir and simmer for 1 minute.
4. **Pour** in the coconut milk, stir once and bring to a simmer. Add the tofu, salt, and pepper. Simmer, stirring occasionally, until the liquid is reduced by half, about 5 minutes.
5. **Remove** from heat then drizzle with lime juice. Garnish with cilantro to serve.

# 54. Spicy Curried Cauliflower and Parsnip Soup

Servings: 3

Preparation time: 15 minutes

Cook time: 48 minutes

Ready in: 1 hour and 3 minutes

## Nutrition Facts

Serving Size 612 g

**Amount Per Serving**

**Calories** 416     Calories from Fat 270

| | % Daily Value* |
|---|---|
| **Total Fat** 30.0g | **46%** |
| Saturated Fat 23.1g | **116%** |
| **Cholesterol** 0mg | **0%** |
| **Sodium** 329mg | **14%** |
| **Total Carbohydrates** 34.0g | **11%** |
| Dietary Fiber 9.5g | **38%** |
| Sugars 12.4g | |
| **Protein** 7.8g | |

Vitamin A 0%    •    Vitamin C 90%

Calcium 7%    •    Iron 19%

**Nutrition Grade B**

* Based on a 2000 calorie diet

## Ingredients

- olive oil spray
- 1 head cauliflower, cut into florets
- 3 medium parsnips, peeled and sliced
- 1 onion, cut into chunks
- 3 cloves garlic, halved
- 5 cups low-sodium vegetable broth
- 1 3/4 cups light coconut milk
- 1 teaspoon honey
- 1 tablespoon red curry paste

## Directions

1. **Preheat** oven to 350 degrees F (175 degrees C).
2. **Place** the cauliflower florets, parsnip, onion, and garlic on a baking sheet. Lightly spray the vegetables with olive oil.

152

3. **Bake** vegetables for 30 minutes, or until golden brown.
4. **Pour** the vegetable broth, coconut milk, honey, and curry paste into a large saucepan over high heat.
5. **Bring** mixture to a boil then add the roasted vegetables. Reduce heat to medium-low and simmer, covered, for 15 minutes.
6. **Pour** soup into a blender and puree until smooth (or depending on desired consistency).
7. **Ladle** soup into bowls and serve.

## 55. Spicy Cilantro Citrus Pork

Servings: 4

Preparation time: 10 minutes

Cook time: 15 minutes

Ready in: 25 minutes

# Nutrition Facts

Serving Size 258 g

**Amount Per Serving**

**Calories** 368        Calories from Fat 106

% Daily Value*

| | |
|---|---|
| **Total Fat** 11.8g | **18%** |
| Saturated Fat 5.8g | **29%** |
| *Trans* Fat 0.1g | |
| **Cholesterol** 166mg | **55%** |
| **Sodium** 607mg | **25%** |
| **Total Carbohydrates** 3.0g | **1%** |
| Dietary Fiber 0.9g | **3%** |
| Sugars 0.6g | |
| **Protein** 59.9g | |

| | | |
|---|---|---|
| Vitamin A 7% | • | Vitamin C 20% |
| Calcium 3% | • | Iron 18% |

**Nutrition Grade B+**

* Based on a 2000 calorie diet

## Ingredients

- 1 teaspoon chili powder
- 1/2 teaspoon crushed red pepper flakes
- 1 teaspoon ground cumin
- 1 teaspoon sea salt

- 1/2 teaspoon freshly ground black pepper
- 4 (1/2-pound) boneless pork loin chops, cut 1 1/4 inches thick
- 1 tablespoon melted coconut oil
- 2 tablespoons finely grated lime zest
- 2 garlic cloves, minced
- 3 tablespoons fresh lime juice
- 2 tablespoons fresh lemon juice
- 3 tablespoons finely chopped cilantro

## Directions

1. **Preheat** the oven to 400 degrees F.
2. **Mix** together the chili powder, red pepper flakes, cumin, salt, and pepper. Season pork chops with the prepared spice mixture.
3. **Heat** the coconut oil in a large ovenproof skillet over high heat. Add the pork chops and brown for 1 minute per side.
4. **Add** the lime zest, garlic, lime juice, lemon juice, and cilantro to the skillet.
5. **Transfer** skillet to oven and roast the chops for 10 minutes.
6. **Place** roasted pork chops onto serving plates and serve.

## 56. Veggie Beef Chili

Servings: 6

Preparation time: 15 minutes

Cook time: 1 hour and 20 minutes

Ready in: 1 hour and 35 minutes

## Nutrition Facts

Serving Size 590 g

**Amount Per Serving**

**Calories** 494      Calories from Fat 187

| | % Daily Value* |
|---|---|
| **Total Fat** 20.8g | **32%** |
| Saturated Fat 12.0g | **60%** |
| Trans Fat 0.0g | |
| **Cholesterol** 136mg | **45%** |
| **Sodium** 519mg | **22%** |
| **Total Carbohydrates** 26.9g | **9%** |
| Dietary Fiber 8.5g | **34%** |
| Sugars 12.1g | |
| **Protein** 52.3g | |

| | | |
|---|---|---|
| Vitamin A 308% | • | Vitamin C 233% |
| Calcium 10% | • | Iron 186% |

**Nutrition Grade A**

* Based on a 2000 calorie diet

## Ingredients

- 2 tablespoons melted coconut oil
- 1 large yellow onion, diced
- 1 clove garlic, chopped
- 2 tablespoons chili powder
- 1 teaspoon cumin
- 1 teaspoon sea salt
- 2 pounds beef stew meat, cut into 1 inch chunks
- 6 cups diced tomatoes
- 1 1/2 cups low-sodium vegetable broth
- 1 cup diced green chilies
- 2 medium zucchini, diced
- 1 bay leaf
- 1 teaspoon organic Italian seasoning

155

- 3 medium carrots, sliced
- 1 large red bell pepper, diced
- 4 large kale leaves, shredded
- chopped fresh cilantro for garnish (optional)
- 1/2 cup coconut cream for garnish (optional)

## Directions

1. **Mix** together the garlic, chili powder, cumin, and salt in a shallow dish. Dredge beef in the spice mixture to coat evenly.
2. **Heat** coconut oil in a large pot over medium-high heat. Stir in onion and cook until slightly browned.
3. **Add** the coated beef to the pot and brown on all sides. Add the diced tomatoes and pour in the vegetable broth.
4. **Stir** in the green chilies, zucchini, Italian seasoning, and bay leaf. Reduce heat to medium. Cook for 40 minutes, stirring occasionally.
5. **Add** carrots and red bell pepper, and cook for 20 minutes. Add the kale leaves and cook for additional 10 minutes.
6. **Serve** topped with cilantro and a dollop of coconut cream.

## 57. Baked Salmon with Coconut Cream Sauce

Servings: 3

Preparation time: 10 minutes

Cook time: 15 minutes

Ready in: 25 minutes

## Nutrition Facts

Serving Size 270 g

**Amount Per Serving**

| | |
|---|---|
| **Calories** 471 | Calories from Fat 287 |

| | % Daily Value* |
|---|---|
| **Total Fat** 31.9g | **49%** |
| Saturated Fat 15.2g | **76%** |
| **Cholesterol** 95mg | **32%** |
| **Sodium** 412mg | **17%** |
| **Total Carbohydrates** 11.3g | **4%** |
| Dietary Fiber 3.6g | **14%** |
| Sugars 4.0g | |
| **Protein** 35.4g | |

| | | |
|---|---|---|
| Vitamin A 3% | • | Vitamin C 41% |
| Calcium 7% | • | Iron 11% |

**Nutrition Grade B**

* Based on a 2000 calorie diet

### Ingredients

- 1 pound salmon fillet
- 1/2 teaspoon sea salt
- 3/4 teaspoon ground nutmeg
- 1/4 teaspoon freshly ground black pepper
- 2 teaspoons melted coconut oil
- 3 cloves garlic, minced
- 1 large red onion, diced
- 1/2 cup coconut milk
- 1 lemon, juiced and zest finely grated
- 2 tablespoons fresh rosemary, chopped

### Directions

1. **Preheat** oven to 350 degrees F.
2. **Season** salmon with salt, nutmeg, and pepper.

3. **Heat** coconut oil in a pan over medium heat. Add the garlic and onions, sauté until onion is soft, about 3 minutes.

4. **Add** the coconut milk, lemon juice and zest; bring to a low boil. Reduce heat then add rosemary. Pour prepared sauce over salmon.

5. **Bake** uncovered for about 10-20 minutes, or until salmon easily flakes with a fork.

## 58. Stir Fried Beef and Lettuce Salad

Servings: 4

Preparation time: 15 minutes

Cook time: 15 minutes

Ready in: 30 minutes

# Nutrition Facts

Serving Size 605 g

**Amount Per Serving**

**Calories** 530  Calories from Fat 226

% Daily Value*

| | % Daily Value* |
|---|---|
| **Total Fat** 25.1g | **39%** |
| Saturated Fat 7.5g | **37%** |
| *Trans* Fat 0.0g | |
| **Cholesterol** 155mg | **52%** |
| **Sodium** 526mg | **22%** |
| **Total Carbohydrates** 22.8g | **8%** |
| Dietary Fiber 9.1g | **36%** |
| Sugars 8.9g | |
| **Protein** 54.1g | |

Vitamin A 128% • Vitamin C 218%

Calcium 18% • Iron 32%

**Nutrition Grade A-**

* Based on a 2000 calorie diet

## Ingredients

- 2 teaspoons melted coconut oil
- 2 cloves garlic, minced
- 1/2 sweet yellow onion, sliced
- 1 chili pepper, minced
- 1 1/2 pounds lean beef tip steak, sliced into thin strips

- 1 tablespoon gluten-free soy sauce
- 2 bell peppers, sliced
- 1 thumb-size ginger, sliced
- 6 ounce snap peas
- 1/2 teaspoon sea salt
- 1/4 teaspoon freshly ground black pepper
- 1 medium head romaine lettuce, chopped
- 15 ounce collard greens, chopped
- 1/2 cup balsamic vinegar
- 3 tablespoons extra virgin olive oil

## Directions

1. **Heat** the coconut oil in a skillet over medium heat. Add the garlic, onion, and chili pepper; sauté until translucent; stirring often. Turn heat up to medium-high.
2. **Stir** in the beef and soy sauce, cook until beef is evenly browned, about 8 to 10 minutes.
3. **Add** the bell peppers, ginger, and snap peas; season with salt and pepper.
4. **Place** beef mixture over collard greens and lettuce.
5. **Drizzle** with balsamic vinegar and olive oil to taste.

## 59. Garlic Chicken with Spicy Mushroom Sauce

Servings: 2

Preparation time: 45 minutes

Cook time: 20 minutes

Ready in: 1 hour and 5 minutes

## Nutrition Facts

Serving Size 408 g

**Amount Per Serving**

**Calories** 537          Calories from Fat 251

|  | % Daily Value* |
|---|---|
| **Total Fat** 27.9g | **43%** |
| Saturated Fat 16.8g | **84%** |
| **Cholesterol** 135mg | **45%** |
| **Sodium** 831mg | **35%** |
| **Total Carbohydrates** 24.6g | **8%** |
| Dietary Fiber 6.4g | **26%** |
| Sugars 13.6g | |
| **Protein** 49.5g | |

| Vitamin A 59% | • | Vitamin C 201% |
|---|---|---|
| Calcium 7% | • | Iron 27% |

**Nutrition Grade B+**

* Based on a 2000 calorie diet

### Ingredients

- 1 pound boneless, skinless chicken breasts, diced
- 2 tablespoons melted coconut oil, divided
- 1/2 teaspoon sea salt
- 1/2 teaspoon ground cayenne pepper
- 1 clove garlic, minced
- 1/4 teaspoon freshly ground black pepper
- 1 medium yellow onion, diced
- 1 cup sundried tomatoes
- 9 cremini mushrooms, sliced
- 2 red bell peppers, sliced
- 1 teaspoon curry powder
- 1/3 cup coconut milk
- 1 lime, juiced
- 1/2 cup chopped fresh cilantro

## Directions

1. **Place** chicken in a large mixing bowl then season with 1 tablespoon coconut oil, salt, cayenne pepper flakes, garlic, and black pepper. Marinate in the refrigerator for at least 30 minutes.

2. **Heat** a medium skillet over medium-high heat. Add the marinated chicken and cook until evenly browned.

3. **Transfer** browned chicken to a plate and set aside. In another skillet, heat the remaining 1 tablespoon coconut oil over medium heat.

4. **Stir** in the onion and cook for 5 minutes, or until translucent. Add the sundried tomatoes and mushrooms, cook until tender.

5. **Add** red bell pepper, curry powder, coconut milk and browned chicken. Stir and cook for 5 minutes more.

6. **Remove** skillet from heat, drizzle with lime juice then stir once. Garnish with chopped cilantro to serve.

## 60. Herbed Black Beans and Quinoa

Servings: 10

Preparation time: 25 minutes

Cook time: 30 minutes

Ready in: 55 minutes

**Nutrition Facts**

Serving Size 350 g

**Amount Per Serving**

Calories 400 — Calories from Fat 48

% Daily Value*

Total Fat 5.4g — 8%

Saturated Fat 2.4g — 12%

Cholesterol 7mg — 2%

Sodium 302mg — 13%

Total Carbohydrates 68.9g — 23%

Dietary Fiber 13.9g — 56%

Sugars 4.7g

Protein 21.2g

Vitamin A 21% • Vitamin C 58%

Calcium 15% • Iron 30%

**Nutrition Grade A**

* Based on a 2000 calorie diet

### Ingredients

- 3/4 cup uncooked quinoa
- 2 cups fresh water
- 1 teaspoon melted coconut oil
- 2 cloves garlic, peeled and chopped
- 1 red bell pepper, chopped
- 1 onion, chopped
- 1 teaspoon ground cumin
- 1/4 teaspoon paprika
- 1/4 teaspoon cayenne pepper
- 1/2 teaspoon sea salt
- 1/4 teaspoon ground black pepper
- 1 1/2 cups organic low-sodium chicken broth
- 1 cup frozen corn kernels

- 1 3/4 cup black beans
- 1/2 cup chopped fresh cilantro
- 1/4 cup grated feta cheese

## Directions

1. **Soak** quinoa in fresh water for 15 minutes then rinse well before cooking.
2. **Heat** coconut oil in a medium saucepan over medium heat. Add garlic, red bell pepper, and onion; sauté until beginning to soften, about 5 minutes.
3. **Stir** in quinoa, cumin, paprika, cayenne pepper, salt, and pepper and cover with chicken broth. Bring the mixture to a boil over medium-high heat.
4. **Cover**, reduce heat to medium-low, and simmer 20 minutes, or until broth is absorbed and quinoa is tender.
5. **Add** the corn, black beans, and ¼ cup cilantro, continue to simmer uncovered until heated through, about 5 minutes.
6. **Ladle** into a bowl and sprinkle with remaining cilantro and cheese.

## 61. Turkey Burgers over Spicy Avocado Slaw

Servings: 5

Preparation time: 15 minutes

Cook time: 10 minutes

Ready in: 25 minutes

**Nutrition Facts**

Serving Size 426 g

**Amount Per Serving**

| | |
|---|---|
| **Calories** 420 | Calories from Fat 250 |

| | % Daily Value* |
|---|---|
| **Total Fat** 27.8g | **43%** |
| Saturated Fat 11.6g | **58%** |
| *Trans* Fat 0.0g | |
| **Cholesterol** 97mg | **32%** |
| **Sodium** 508mg | **21%** |
| **Total Carbohydrates** 24.9g | **8%** |
| Dietary Fiber 11.1g | **44%** |
| Sugars 10.4g | |
| **Protein** 23.6g | |

| | | |
|---|---|---|
| Vitamin A 108% | • | Vitamin C 246% |
| Calcium 11% | • | Iron 20% |

**Nutrition Grade B**

* Based on a 2000 calorie diet

### Ingredients

*Burger:*

- 1 pound lean ground turkey
- 1 egg
- 1 red onion, minced
- 3 chipotle peppers, diced
- 1/2 red bell pepper, diced
- 1 teaspoon ground cumin
- 1/2 teaspoon ground red pepper
- 2 tablespoons chopped fresh parsley
- 1/2 teaspoon sea salt
- 1/4 teaspoon ground black pepper
- 2 tablespoons melted coconut oil

*Spicy Avocado Slaw:*

- 2 carrots, shredded
- 2 avocados
- 1 teaspoon raw honey
- 1 tablespoon melted coconut oil
- 1 teaspoon lime juice
- 1 teaspoon apple cider vinegar
- 1 teaspoon ground cilantro
- 1/2 teaspoon crushed red pepper
- 1/2 teaspoon sea salt
- 1/4 teaspoon ground black pepper
- 2 tablespoons chopped green onions
- 1 small head of cabbage or bag of cabbage, chopped

## Directions

1. **Combine** all ingredients (leaving 1 tablespoon of coconut oil) for the burger in a large mixing bowl. Form mixture into small patties.
2. **Heat** coconut oil in a large skillet over medium heat. Add patties and cook on both sides for about 3 to 5 minutes.
3. **Place** all your ingredients for the slaw (except the cabbage) in a food processor or blender and pulse until smooth.
4. **Pour** your avocado mixture over the cabbage and toss to combine.
5. **Place** avocado slaw onto serving plates and top with the burger patties.

## 62. Fish Sticks with Coconut Aminos Mayo

Servings: 6
Preparation time: 10 minutes
Cook time: 10 minutes
Ready in: 20 minutes

## Nutrition Facts

Serving Size 164 g

**Amount Per Serving**

**Calories** 359      Calories from Fat 252

| | % Daily Value* |
|---|---|
| **Total Fat** 28.0g | **43%** |
| Saturated Fat 16.9g | **84%** |
| *Trans* Fat 0.0g | |
| **Cholesterol** 48mg | **16%** |
| **Sodium** 557mg | **23%** |
| **Total Carbohydrates** 4.7g | **2%** |
| Sugars 1.0g | |
| **Protein** 23.5g | |

| | | |
|---|---|---|
| Vitamin A 4% | • | Vitamin C 3% |
| Calcium 5% | • | Iron 7% |

**Nutrition Grade C-**
* Based on a 2000 calorie diet

### Ingredients

- 2 organic free-range eggs, whisked
- 1/2 cup blanched almond flour
- 1/2 teaspoon paprika
- 1/4 cup dried basil
- 3 cloves garlic, finely chopped
- 1 teaspoon sea salt
- 1/4 teaspoon freshly ground black pepper
- 1/2 cup coconut oil
- 1 pound white fish, cut into 1x5-inch pieces
- 1/4 cup coconut aminos
- 1/2 cup gluten-free low-fat mayonnaise

## Directions

1. **Whisk** eggs in a medium bowl. In another bowl, mix the almond flour, paprika, basil, garlic, salt, and pepper.
2. **Dip** fish sticks in egg, then in flour mixture to coat evenly; place coated sticks in a plate.
3. **Heat** coconut oil in a large skillet over medium high heat. Add the fish sticks and cook for 2-3 minutes on each side until well-browned. Leave enough room around fish sticks so that they aren't overcrowded.
4. **Drain** fish sticks on paper towels in a plate.
5. **Whisk** together the coconut aminos and mayonnaise in a bowl.
6. **Serve** fish sticks with mayonnaise mixture.

## 63. Turkey Stuffed Sweet Potatoes

Servings: 3

Preparation time: 15 minutes

Cook time: 40 minutes

Ready in: 55 minutes

**Nutrition Facts**

Serving Size 321 g

Amount Per Serving

Calories 556 — Calories from Fat 226

% Daily Value*

| | % Daily Value* |
|---|---|
| Total Fat 25.2g | 39% |
| Saturated Fat 9.2g | 46% |
| Trans Fat 0.0g | |
| Cholesterol 154mg | 51% |
| Sodium 1009mg | 42% |
| Total Carbohydrates 37.3g | 12% |
| Dietary Fiber 6.3g | 25% |
| Sugars 4.8g | |
| Protein 44.0g | |

| | | |
|---|---|---|
| Vitamin A 14% | • | Vitamin C 62% |
| Calcium 8% | • | Iron 23% |

**Nutrition Grade B-**

* Based on a 2000 calorie diet

### Ingredients

- 2 large sweet potatoes
- 1 tablespoon melted coconut oil
- 1 clove garlic, minced
- 1 yellow onion, diced
- 1 pound ground turkey
- 1/4 cup red hot sauce
- 2 teaspoons chili powder
- 1 teaspoon crushed cayenne pepper
- 1 teaspoon garlic powder
- 1 teaspoon onion powder
- 1/2 teaspoon ground cinnamon
- 1/2 teaspoon dried oregano
- 1/2 teaspoon sea salt

168

- 1/4 teaspoon ground black pepper
- 1 teaspoon raw honey

## Directions

1. **Preheat** oven to 425 degrees F.
2. **Halve** sweet potatoes lengthwise and place them face down on a cookie sheet.
3. **Cook** in the preheated oven for about 25-30 minutes.
4. **Heat** coconut oil in a skillet over medium-high heat. Add garlic and onions, sauté until onions are translucent.
5. **Stir** in the ground turkey, spices, and salt; cook until turkey is no longer pink.
6. **Remove** sweet potatoes from the oven and use a large spoon to scoop out the insides, leaving a 1/2 inch thick layer in potato shell.
7. **Place** the scooped flesh of the sweet potatoes directly into the skillet. Add honey and mix thoroughly.
8. **Scoop** out the turkey mixture and place into the sweet potato skins. Place the stuffed sweet potatoes back onto the cookie sheet.
9. **Bake** in the oven for 3-5 minutes.

# DESSERT AND SNACK

## 64. Almond Coconut Macaroons

Servings: 5

Preparation time: 40 minutes

Cook time: 10 minutes

Ready in: 50 minutes

**Nutrition Facts**

Serving Size 76 g

| | |
|---|---|
| **Amount Per Serving** | |
| **Calories** 349 | Calories from Fat 252 |
| | **% Daily Value\*** |
| **Total Fat** 28.1g | **43%** |
| Saturated Fat 21.4g | **107%** |
| *Trans* Fat 0.0g | |
| **Cholesterol** 0mg | **0%** |
| **Sodium** 128mg | **5%** |
| **Total Carbohydrates** 25.9g | **9%** |
| Dietary Fiber 1.4g | **6%** |
| Sugars 16.8g | |
| **Protein** 5.9g | |
| Vitamin A 0% • | Vitamin C 0% |
| Calcium 3% • | Iron 7% |
| **Nutrition Grade F** | |
| \* Based on a 2000 calorie diet | |

## Ingredients

- 2 large egg whites
- 1/4 cup raw honey
- 1 teaspoon pure vanilla extract
- 1 teaspoon ground cinnamon
- 1/4 teaspoon sea salt
- 2 1/2 cups unsweetened coconut flakes
- 1/2 cup almonds, chopped
- 1 cup cold water

## Directions

1. **Preheat** the oven to 350 degrees F. Line a baking sheet with parchment paper.

2. **Whisk** together the egg whites, honey, and vanilla in a bowl. Stir in the cinnamon, salt and coconut flakes.

3. **Chill** the batter for 30 minutes then stir a few times after removing from the fridge.

4. **Dip** a 2-tablespoon scoop in cold water, and then scoop out the batter onto prepared baking sheet.

5. **Bake** the macaroons for 10-12 minutes, until golden brown. Allow macaroons to cool slightly on the baking sheet, and then transfer to wire rack to cool completely before serving.

## 65. Berry Hazelnut Parfait with Coconut Vanilla Ice Cream

Servings: 6
Ready in: 50 minutes

# Nutrition Facts

Serving Size 220 g

**Amount Per Serving**

**Calories** 407            Calories from Fat 242

% **Daily Value\***

| | |
|---|---|
| **Total Fat** 26.9g | **41%** |
| Saturated Fat 17.5g | **87%** |
| *Trans* Fat 0.0g | |
| **Cholesterol** 0mg | **0%** |
| **Sodium** 14mg | **1%** |
| **Total Carbohydrates** 43.8g | **15%** |
| Dietary Fiber 5.2g | **21%** |
| Sugars 30.5g | |
| **Protein** 4.5g | |

| | | |
|---|---|---|
| Vitamin A 1% | • | Vitamin C 61% |
| Calcium 4% | • | Iron 13% |

**Nutrition Grade C-**
\* Based on a 2000 calorie diet

## Ingredients

*Ice Cream:*

- 2 cups ice cold organic full-fat coconut milk
- 1/2 cup raw honey
- 2 teaspoons pure vanilla extract

172

*Parfait:*

- 1 1/2 cups fresh strawberries, sliced
- 2 cups fresh blueberries
- 1 lemon, juiced
- 1 tablespoon raw honey
- 1 teaspoon ground cinnamon
- 1 cup hazelnuts, chopped

## Directions

1. **Combine** the coconut milk, honey, and vanilla in a blender. Cover and blend on High until smooth and frothy.
2. **Transfer** mixture into a frozen ice cream bowl, cover, and start ice cream maker to churn it. Transfer to a freezer safe container and freeze for 30 minutes.
3. **Chill** six parfait glasses.
4. **Toss** together the strawberries and blueberries in a bowl. Drizzle with lemon juice and honey then sprinkle with cinnamon.
5. **Layer** the berries, hazelnuts and coconut vanilla ice cream in parfait glasses.

## 66. Choco Banana Ice Cream

Servings: 5

Ready in: 1 hour and 10 minutes

**Nutrition Facts**

Serving Size 234 g

**Amount Per Serving**

| Calories 474 | Calories from Fat 269 |
|---|---|

| | % Daily Value* |
|---|---|
| **Total Fat** 29.9g | **46%** |
| Saturated Fat 13.6g | **68%** |
| **Cholesterol** 0mg | **0%** |
| **Sodium** 9mg | **0%** |
| **Total Carbohydrates** 53.7g | **18%** |
| Dietary Fiber 6.3g | **25%** |
| Sugars 32.8g | |
| **Protein** 7.1g | |

| Vitamin A 2% | • | Vitamin C 23% |
|---|---|---|
| Calcium 6% | • | Iron 12% |

**Nutrition Grade C-**

* Based on a 2000 calorie diet

### Ingredients

- 6 ripe bananas, peeled, sliced and frozen
- 1 cup full-fat coconut milk
- 1/4 cup almond butter
- 1 teaspoon pure vanilla extract
- 2 tablespoon raw honey
- 1/2 cup grated dark chocolate chips
- 1/2 cup sliced pecans

### Directions

1. **Place** bananas in a food processor or blender and puree until smooth.
2. **Stir** in coconut milk, almond butter, vanilla, honey, and chocolate chips; blend until smooth.
3. **Fold** in pecans.
4. **Pour** mixture into a freezable container and freeze for 1 hour before serving.

# 67. Peanut Butter Chocolate Chip Cookies

Servings: 4

Preparation time: 15 minutes

Cook time: 15 minutes

Ready in: 30 minutes

## Nutrition Facts

Serving Size 112 g

**Amount Per Serving**

**Calories** 419　　　　Calories from Fat 277

% Daily Value*

| | |
|---|---|
| **Total Fat** 30.7g | **47%** |
| Saturated Fat 11.3g | **56%** |
| *Trans* Fat 0.0g | |
| **Cholesterol** 41mg | **14%** |
| **Sodium** 305mg | **13%** |
| **Total Carbohydrates** 31.3g | **10%** |
| Dietary Fiber 3.2g | **13%** |
| Sugars 24.9g | |
| **Protein** 11.9g | |

Vitamin A 1%　　•　　Vitamin C 0%

Calcium 5%　　•　　Iron 8%

**Nutrition Grade D**

* Based on a 2000 calorie diet

## Ingredients

- 1 1/4 cups almond flour
- 1/4 teaspoon baking soda
- 1/8 teaspoon sea salt
- 1 teaspoon ground cinnamon
- 1 egg
- 1/4 cup of raw honey
- 1 teaspoon pure vanilla extract
- 1/2 cup creamy peanut butter
- 2 tablespoons melted coconut oil
- 1/4 cup dark chocolate chips

## Directions

1. **Preheat** oven to 325 degrees F. Line a cookie sheet with parchment paper.

2. **Mix** together the flour, baking soda, salt, and cinnamon in a large mixing bowl. In a separate bowl, whisk together the egg, honey, vanilla, peanut butter, and coconut oil.

3. **Pour** the egg mixture into the flour mixture and blend well. Fold in the chocolate chips.

4. **Scoop** out batter (about 3 tablespoons per cookie) and roll into balls. Place onto the prepared cookie sheet and flatten lightly in the center, arrange 2 inches apart.

5. **Bake** for 10-15 minutes.

## 68. Coconut Cream Cake

Servings: 10

Preparation time: 1 hour and 15 minutes

Cook time: 30 minutes

Ready in: 1 hour and 45 minutes

## Nutrition Facts

Serving Size 213 g

**Amount Per Serving**

| | |
|---|---|
| **Calories** 601 | Calories from Fat 275 |

| | % Daily Value* |
|---|---|
| **Total Fat** 30.6g | **47%** |
| Saturated Fat 23.8g | **119%** |
| Trans Fat 0.0g | |
| **Cholesterol** 84mg | **28%** |
| **Sodium** 352mg | **15%** |
| **Total Carbohydrates** 76.1g | **25%** |
| Dietary Fiber 1.8g | **7%** |
| Sugars 51.5g | |
| **Protein** 8.7g | |

| | | |
|---|---|---|
| Vitamin A 8% | • | Vitamin C 5% |
| Calcium 20% | • | Iron 12% |

**Nutrition Grade D-**

* Based on a 2000 calorie diet

### Ingredients

- 3 eggs
- 1 cup water
- 1/3 cup melted coconut oil, plus extra amount for greasing

- 1/2 teaspoon pure vanilla extract
- 1 (18 ounce) package gluten-free white cake mix
- 1 3/4 cup coconut cream
- 1 3/4 cup fat-free sweetened condensed milk
- 1 cup heavy whipping cream
- 1 tablespoon raw honey
- 1 teaspoon ground cinnamon
- 1 cup coconut flakes

## Directions

1. **Preheat** oven to 350 degrees F (175 degrees C). Grease a 9x13 inch baking pan with coconut oil and flour with a little amount of the white cake mix.
2. **Beat** together the eggs, water, coconut oil, and vanilla in a large bowl until smooth. Stir in the cake mix until blended. Pour mixture into the prepared baking pan.
3. **Bake** for 30 minutes, or until a toothpick inserted into the cake comes out clean.
4. **Stir** together the coconut cream with condensed milk in a medium bowl until smooth. Remove pan from the oven then pour milk mixture over the cake. Refrigerate for 1 hour.
5. **Whisk** together the cream, honey, and cinnamon until soft peaks form. Spread mixture over cooled cake and sprinkle coconut flakes over the top.

## 69. Coconut Blueberry Cupcakes

Servings: 3

Preparation time: 15 minutes

Cook time: 20 minutes

Ready in: 35 minutes

**Nutrition Facts**

Serving Size 208 g

**Amount Per Serving**

| | |
|---|---|
| **Calories** 527 | Calories from Fat 189 |
| | **% Daily Value*** |
| **Total Fat** 21.0g | **32%** |
| Saturated Fat 7.3g | **36%** |
| *Trans* Fat 0.0g | |
| **Cholesterol** 248mg | **83%** |
| **Sodium** 506mg | **21%** |
| **Total Carbohydrates** 70.4g | **23%** |
| Dietary Fiber 10.8g | **43%** |
| Sugars 52.8g | |
| **Protein** 15.3g | |

| | | |
|---|---|---|
| Vitamin A 7% | • | Vitamin C 10% |
| Calcium 9% | • | Iron 23% |

**Nutrition Grade D+**

* Based on a 2000 calorie diet

### Ingredients

- 1/2 cup coconut flour
- 1/2 cup coconut flakes
- 1 tablespoon gluten-free cornstarch
- 1/2 teaspoon baking soda
- 1/4 teaspoon sea salt
- 1/2 teaspoon ground cinnamon
- 4 large eggs
- 1/2 cup raw honey
- 1 tablespoon pure vanilla extract
- 1/2 cup fresh blueberries, mashed
- 1/2 cup almonds, chopped
- 1 tablespoon lemon zest, finely chopped

## Directions

1. **Preheat** oven to 350 degrees F. Line a 6-cup muffin tin with paper liners.
2. **Mix** together the coconut flour, coconut flakes, cornstarch, baking soda, salt, and cinnamon in a medium bowl.
3. **Whisk** together the eggs, honey, and vanilla in a large bowl.
4. **Add** the flour mixture into the egg mixture and blend well. Stir in the mashed blueberries, almonds, and lemon zest.
5. **Divide** and scoop ¼ cup of batter into each muffin cup.
6. **Bake** for 20-25 minutes. Let cool and serve.

## 70. Fresh Pumpkin Squares

Servings: 3

Preparation time: 20 minutes

Cook time: 25 minutes

Ready in: 45 minutes

# Nutrition Facts

Serving Size 378 g

**Amount Per Serving**

**Calories** 495          Calories from Fat 223

% Daily Value*

| | |
|---|---|
| **Total Fat** 24.7g | **38%** |
| Saturated Fat 17.9g | **90%** |
| **Cholesterol** 218mg | **73%** |
| **Sodium** 777mg | **32%** |
| **Total Carbohydrates** 67.6g | **23%** |
| Dietary Fiber 5.2g | **21%** |
| Sugars 56.4g | |
| **Protein** 9.5g | |

| | | |
|---|---|---|
| Vitamin A 514% | • | Vitamin C 13% |
| Calcium 24% | • | Iron 24% |

**Nutrition Grade C+**

* Based on a 2000 calorie diet

## Ingredients

- 4 eggs

- 2 cups fresh pumpkin puree
- 1/2 cup raw honey
- 1 tablespoon pure maple syrup
- 1/4 cup coconut oil, plus extra amount for greasing
- 2 cups almond flour
- 3 1/2 teaspoons pumpkin pie spice
- 1 teaspoon baking soda
- 2 teaspoons gluten-free baking powder
- 1/2 teaspoon unrefined sea salt

## Directions

1. **Preheat** oven to 350 degrees F. Grease a 9x13 inch baking pan with coconut oil.
2. **Whisk** together the eggs, pumpkin puree, honey, maple syrup, and coconut oil until smooth.
3. **Mix** together the flour, pumpkin pie spice, baking soda, baking powder, and salt then stir into the pumpkin mixture. Transfer batter into the baking pan.
4. **Bake** for 25 to 30 minutes. Cool, cut into squares, and serve.

## 71. Coconut Ambrosia Salad

Servings: 4

Ready in: 1 hour and 15 minutes

# Nutrition Facts

Serving Size 453 g

**Amount Per Serving**

**Calories** 574          Calories from Fat 292

                                    **% Daily Value***

| | |
|---|---|
| **Total Fat** 32.4g | **50%** |
| Saturated Fat 19.1g | **95%** |
| *Trans* Fat 0.0g | |
| **Cholesterol** 5mg | **2%** |
| **Sodium** 38mg | **2%** |
| **Total Carbohydrates** 57.1g | **19%** |
| Dietary Fiber 9.4g | **38%** |
| Sugars 30.6g | |
| **Protein** 15.2g | |

| | | |
|---|---|---|
| Vitamin A 12% | • | Vitamin C 62% |
| Calcium 34% | • | Iron 43% |

**Nutrition Grade C+**

* Based on a 2000 calorie diet

## Ingredients

- 1 1/2 cup peeled mandarin orange segments
- 1 cup fresh pineapple chunks
- 1 cup sliced almonds
- 3 cups coconut cream
- 2 cups shredded unsweetened coconut
- 1 tablespoon pure vanilla extract
- 1/2 cup coconut milk
- 1/2 cup blueberries
- 1/2 cup cherries

### Directions

1. **Combine** the oranges, pineapple, almonds, coconut cream, shredded coconut, vanilla, and coconut milk.
2. **Toss** to combine and chill 1 hour before serving.
3. **Garnish** with blueberries and cherries to serve.

## 72. Carrot Hazelnut Soufflé

Servings: 5

Preparation time: 10 minutes

Cook time: 45 minutes

Ready in: 55 minutes

**Nutrition Facts**

Serving Size 243 g

**Amount Per Serving**

| | |
|---|---|
| **Calories** 443 | Calories from Fat 240 |

**% Daily Value\***

| | |
|---|---|
| **Total Fat** 26.7g | **41%** |
| Saturated Fat 9.3g | **47%** |
| *Trans* Fat 0.0g | |
| **Cholesterol** 0mg | **0%** |
| **Sodium** 167mg | **7%** |
| **Total Carbohydrates** 49.1g | **16%** |
| Dietary Fiber 8.7g | **35%** |
| Sugars 35.8g | |
| **Protein** 9.9g | |

| | |
|---|---|
| Vitamin A 303% | Vitamin C 16% |
| Calcium 13% | Iron 13% |

**Nutrition Grade B-**

\* Based on a 2000 calorie diet

### Ingredients

- 1 pounds carrots, chopped
- 1/3 cup organic coconut butter, melted
- 1/2 cup raw honey
- 3 tablespoons almond flour
- 1 teaspoon gluten-free baking powder
- 1 teaspoon pure maple syrup
- 2 tablespoons fresh orange juice
- 3 eggs, beaten

- 1 teaspoon ground cinnamon
- 1 teaspoon freshly grated nutmeg
- 1 cup toasted hazelnuts, chopped

## Directions
1. **Preheat** oven to 350 degrees f (175 degrees c).
2. **Add** carrots to a large pot of salted water. Cook for 15 minutes, or until tender; drain, cool, and mash.
3. **Combine** mashed carrots with the remaining ingredients (except the hazelnuts) in a 2-quart casserole dish. Spread hazelnuts evenly on top.
4. **Bake** for 30 minutes.

## 73. Peach and Cherry Cobbler

Servings: 5

Preparation time: 15 minutes

Cook time: 50 minutes

Ready in: 1 hour and 5 minutes

# Nutrition Facts

Serving Size 230 g

**Amount Per Serving**

**Calories** 302　　　　　Calories from Fat 73

% **Daily Value***

| | |
|---|---|
| **Total Fat** 8.1g | **12%** |
| Saturated Fat 6.5g | **33%** |
| *Trans* Fat 0.0g | |
| **Cholesterol** 2mg | **1%** |
| **Sodium** 193mg | **8%** |
| **Total Carbohydrates** 76.0g | **25%** |
| Dietary Fiber 5.1g | **20%** |
| Sugars 10.3g | |
| **Protein** 4.5g | |

Vitamin A 8%　　•　　Vitamin C 10%

Calcium 10%　　•　　Iron 5%

**Nutrition Grade C**

* Based on a 2000 calorie diet

## Ingredients
- 1/4 cup coconut butter

- 3/4 cup gluten-free all-purpose flour
- 3/4 cup stevia
- 1 teaspoon gluten-free baking powder
- 2 teaspoons pumpkin pie spice
- 1/4 teaspoon sea salt
- 3/4 cup low-fat milk
- 1 teaspoon pure maple syrup
- 1 cup fresh peaches, sliced
- 1 cup cherries
- 1 tablespoon raw honey

### Directions
1. **Preheat** oven to 350 degrees F.
2. **Melt** the coconut butter in a 9-inch round pan in the oven. Remove pan from oven.
3. **Whisk** together the flour, stevia, baking powder, pumpkin pie spice, and salt in a bowl.
4. **Pour in** the milk and maple syrup, whisk until smooth. Transfer batter into pan.
5. **Spread** peaches and cherries over batter then drizzle with honey.
6. **Bake** for 50 to 60 minutes, or until evenly browned on top.

## Books by Maggie Fitzgerald

Coconut Flour! 47+ Irresistible Recipes for Baking with Coconut Flour

Almond Flour! Gluten Free & Paleo Diet Cookbook

The Gluten Free Diet Quick Start Guide

Simple Gluten Free & Paleo Bread

Real Coconut Oil Results

www.amazon.com/author/donatellagiordano

## About Donatella Giordano

In addition to being an acclaimed chef, Donatella Giordano is considered an expert in the field of gourmet, gluten-free and paleo cooking.

Through her tasty natural gluten-free recipes, she has gradually managed to win over her husband, three kids and two chocolate labradors, all of whom now love their healthy diets and lifestyles.

In her spare time she can be found around Palo Alto, scouring farmers' markets, hiking or cycling with the family.

# Exclusive Bonus Download: Coconut Oil - The Healthy Fat

Download your bonus, please visit the download link above from your PC or MAC. To open PDF files, visit http://get.adobe.com/reader/ to download the reader if it's not already installed on your PC or Mac. To open ZIP files, you may need to download WinZip from http://www.winzip.com. This download is for PC or Mac ONLY and might not be downloadable to kindle.

Coconut oil the complete natural health guide!

Find out the health benefits of coconut oil today!

Find out how coconut oil can, cure common illnesses saving you hundreds in doctors' fees, help you lose weight without losing the great taste of your favorite foods and much, much more!

Coconut oil has long been held in high repute by natural health specialists and doctors from a massively diverse range of countries. Western medicine has been slow to catch on to the health benefits of coconut oil but cutting edge research is finally catching up to what eastern doctors have known for centuries; COCONUT OIL IS GOOD FOR YOU!

Whilst many claims are made about the benefits of coconut oil in your diet and as a topical skin treatment finding good information on the wide range of benefits coconut oil can have for you can be incredibly time consuming and tricky.

**Visit the URL above to download this guide and start improving your health NOW**

# One Last Thing...

Thank you so much for reading my book. I hope you really liked it. As you probably know, many people look at the reviews on Amazon before they decide to purchase a book. If you liked the book, could you please take a minute to leave a review with your feedback? 60 seconds is all I'm asking for, and it would mean the world to me.

Donatella Giordano

**NaturalWay**
Publishing

Atlanta, Georgia USA

5381672R00107

Printed in Great Britain
by Amazon.co.uk, Ltd.,
Marston Gate.